MW01051108

ESSENTIAL SKILLS

FOR

HIGHLY SUCCESSFUL

YOUTHS

Nurturing Competitive Leaders of the 21st Century and beyond

(For High School and Tertiary Level Students)

Carolyne Mande Lunga

Printed 2019
©2019 CM Lunga
ISBN: 978 0 7978 0535 4

Cover design by Thabo Mkhatshwa: anointedtymng@gmail.com

Proof Reader Adiele Dube
This book has been reviewed by independent reviewers
For Enquiries: carolynem05@gmail.com
© All rights reserved

No part of this book may be reproduced in any form or by any
means mechanical or electronic, including recordings or tape
recordings and photocopying without the prior permission of the
author, excluding fair quotations for purposes of research or review.

Printed by Novus Print

About the Author

Carolyne Mande Lunga is a highly motivated career development coach with vast experience in teaching at university and working with young people in Zimbabwe, South Africa and Eswatini. Currently, Lecturer of Journalism and Mass Communication (JMC) at the University of Eswatini (UNESWA), Lunga is passionate about youth development. She has qualifications in Journalism and Media Studies and Higher Education from National University of Science and Technology (NUST) in Zimbabwe and Rhodes University in South Africa. Her research interests include critical skills, media representation, contemporary trends in journalism, first year learning and social media and development.

Lunga, who is the winner of the 2013 UNESCO Asia–Pacific Film/Article e-Contest running under the theme: "Skills for Better Life," produced an article with the title *Critical Skills of the 21st Century*, deemed to be among the best out of 198 submissions received from 19 countries. The then Zimbabwean, Higher and Tertiary Education, Science and Technology Development Permanent Secretary Dr Washington Mbizvo, congratulated Lunga for her "intellectual prowess, creativity and originality in response to the article". Through this book, Lunga takes the article to a higher level by motivating and appealing to youths to acquire critical skills which will enable them to contribute to solving the world's problems in an increasingly interdependent world. The purpose of the book is to nurture leaders of tomorrow who are purposeful, visionary and successful.

Dedication

To Emma, Emily and Precious and all young people and individuals seeking success.

Acknowledgements

I wish to express my gratitude to the people who contributed immensely in the content review process. Dr. Phindile Alice Dlamini, for her honest and insightful criticism of sections of the book.

Dr. Eunice Mthethwa-Kunene for her guidance and support and ensuring the successful production of this book. Thank you also for all the links to key people in various sectors of education and publishing.

Dr. Gciniwe Nsibande for the inspiration and conversations we had on issues affecting youths and providing key contacts who would ensure the book meets required standards. Dr. Boyie, S. Dlamini, Dr. Francis F. Lukhele, Dr. Karen Fereirra-Meyers, Dr. Gaolathe Tsheboeng, Dr. Racheal Mafumbate, Zanele Ncube, Faith Madlala, Adiele Dube, Norbert Mungwini, thank you for the constructive comments important for improving the chapters of the book.

Thank you to Professor Francis L.C. Rakotsoane for the initial and follow up discussions that led to the production of this book. Thank you also for doing the overall editing, the inspiration and making me realise that it is possible to produce a book. Thabo Mzileni thank you for the editorial support. Nompilo Mavimbela thank you for your presence during the entire period of crafting the manuscript.

Lastly, I wish thank all my teachers who have shaped me into the person I am today. To my parents Nelson and Sheilla who taught me to value education, thank you. The person most responsible for this book becoming a reality is my husband Adiele, who supports all my academic endeavours.

SECTION ONE: THINKING SKILLS

Chapter One: Critical Thinking

Chapter Two: Problem Solving

Chapter Three: Creativity and Innovation

Chapter Four: Emotional Intelligence

Chapter Five: Decision Making

SECTION TWO: ACTION/CREATIVITY SKILLS

Chapter Six: Communication

Chapter Seven: Media and Information Literacy

Chapter Eight: Entrepreneurship

Chapter Nine: Financial Literacy

SECTION THREE: SKILLS FOR LIVING IN THE WORLD

Chapter Ten: Lifelong learning

Chapter Eleven: Leadership

Chapter Twelve: Stress Management

SECTION FOUR: PERSONAL SKILLS

Chapter Thirteen: Flexibility and Adaptability

Chapter Fourteen: Being Positive at all times

Chapter Fifteen: Physical Fitness, Wellness and Living a Healthy Lifestyle

SECTION FIVE: SOCIAL SKILLS

SECTION SIX: INFORMATION COMMUNICATION AND TECHNOLOGY (ICT) SKILLS

Chapter Twenty: **Using various ICT tools**

SECTION SEVEN: CVS,   RESUMES,   PERSONAL STATEMENTS AND COVER LETTERS

Chapter Twenty-One: **Writing Winning CVs**

Chapter Twenty-Two: **Writing a Winning Resume**

Chapter Twenty-Seven: Other Important things to be Done

Appendices

Introduction

Growing up in a neither poor nor rich family, I was taught about hard work, which has brought me to where I am today. My parents and grandmothers preached education to us (myself, brother and sister). We were continually told that the only avenue to success was to be educated, get a good job and buy a dream house and car. "Carolyne, you need to work hard at school. Education is what you need for success," my grannies would always say. It surprised me how they spoke so highly about education yet they themselves were not that much educated. One thing for sure, they loved their Bibles and they read them at all times.

We took advice from our parents and grannies and did our best. While not all of the above has happened to all 3 of us yet, 'success' has been achieved. My brother Nqobile failed at school. He only managed to get 4 O' Levels after several sittings. I saw him try and fail and try again. At primary school he was always at the bottom of the class yet when he went on the sports track, he was always ahead of other athletes. He was a good athlete but he did not pursue athletics. He acquired skills in driving and is a long distance truck driver today.

I have a job which enables me to contribute in the area I am passionate about, Journalism and also be able to cover my needs. To be honest, it has not been easy to get to where I am today. I, Sithabile and Nqobile continue to persevere and look forward. We have fallen and risen, again and again and sometimes have been lifted and encouraged by others. When I look back, look at myself and others around me, including Sithabile and Nqobile, I realise that it is not only education that brings about success to individuals. There are a host of critical skills that are important for young people to be highly successful and to make a meaningful contribution to this world. These skills are nurtured at school and at home yet sometimes these

1

two places do not adequately equip young people with the skills to survive and contribute to this challenging world of the 21st Century.

Both my grannies have passed on. We were all shattered when they passed on but we have hope that one day we will see them. My parents are both alive and I am grateful for what they have taught me and how they always encourage me and my siblings to do better. The song of education which my grandmothers sung continues to play in my ears. "Education will unlock great doors for you, continue to learn," my parents would say always. I miss the advice about life that came from these elderly women. Today, I am a parent myself. If I am not working or looking after my children, I reflect on life situations. I ask myself questions regarding education, the meaning of life and what the purpose of the individual really is in society. I think about the advice that came from my grannies, parents and all the people I have met in my life and in doing so I have gained valuable insight into the power and effect of one's thoughts in one's life.

I remember being bullied when I was in the second grade at primary school and how that made me fear going to back until my granny discovered that I was not going to school and took me there so that the issue could be brought to the teacher's attention and the responsible children be brought to book. There were a number of bullies at the school and it is scary to think today that at such a lower grade, there are children that exercise violence on others. Children are innocent and vulnerable and they need to be taught good habits at an early age. They should not be subjected to violence or immoral behaviour as it can affect their growth and this includes not subjecting them to content of a violent, sexual or graphic nature on television and the internet. Being aware of one's environment is important to both the young and old. Some programmes which parents watch on television, display nudity, sex and objectify and stereotype certain social groups particularly women and minority ethnicities. It is unsafe to let children select and watch cartoons

2

online unsupervised. Criminals have encroached into cartoons and altered the content with the intention of corrupting children's thoughts and behaviour. I have come across the altered version of the children's cartoon *Peppa Pig* online. In it, Peppa chased other children with a very large knife. I got scared and began to worry about children who innocently get exposed to such criminally altered cartoons. Parental guidance is required when it comes to the media, both traditional and newer forms, with regards to what children have access to. The warnings on television about parental guidance are important to take note of in order to protect minors from indecent content, strong and hateful language, sex and violence.

I will never forget my high school days. The teachers were very committed and always emphasised hard work. Some of my teachers are still alive today and are at the same schools. Some have advanced and changed careers and it is always good to meet them and be reminded of the times of old. I remember the good and bad times. I remember how I was very shy in all my years of high school. My classmates teased me because of my oversized blazer and they nicknamed me "Nkalakatha" which means very big. It was during the days when the late South African artist, Mandoza's song, "Nkalakatha" was very popular. So other classmates would even call me "Mandoza" if they wished. The oversized blazer killed my confidence. I remained glued to the chair during break and lunch times because I was afraid of facing other learners in the school who would laugh at it. I did not tell my parents about all what was happening at school. When I look back, I realise that I should have been more open to my parents about how I felt about the blazer. I should have cast out all the fears I developed due to the piece of clothing I wore everyday to school. The other learners acted unfairly towards me. I have come to realise that it is not good to judge and laugh at other people as it can lower their self esteem and confidence.

Apart from the blazer story, I remember some good moments at school. I remember the Mathematics teacher, Mrs Noma Ndlela, who easily solved difficult mathematics questions. She was soft and humble and accommodated everyone in the class. There were some learners who became popular for bunking Mathematics. No one bunked Science lessons because we were all scared of Mr Simon Moyo, who used a stick to discipline us and most learners enjoyed the practical work. The same applied to Food and Nutrition, we enjoyed the cooking sessions and on the weeks we did practical work, we gained a lot of new friends from our class and other classes. But we never thought much about it. It was just great to share the food. At my school, practical subjects were divided according to sex just like in many other schools. Girls had to 'choose' between Food and Nutrition and Fashion and Fabrics while boys did Woodwork or Metalwork. I think about it today and come to the conclusion that this kind of dividing practicals on the basis of sex was unfair. Young people should be exposed to a wide range of practical subjects so that they are not limited in their life. Skills coming from the four practical subjects and others are important for would be entrepreneurs and all young people need them regardless of gender or other demographic information.

I remember my Ndebele teacher at A' Level, Mrs Maureen Sibanda. She made us to admire African Languages and to love the Humanities or Arts subjects. Other classmates in Commerce and the Sciences always looked down upon us. They would ask questions such as "Are you serious that you enrolled for A-Level to study isiNdebele or History? Or "What career are you going to do with IsiNdebele? These questions were baffling. Thanks to Mrs Sibanda, who inspired confidence in us. We were proud to tell them that the Ndebele subject was equally as important as Maths, Geography, Physics and Chemistry and that there were a number of career options available for people who have studied Arts subjects. Ndebele and English subjects helped us develop critical thinking skills which are important in today's world. Today, I know that all subjects are important. In fact there is no subject that is superior to another. Mathematics, English, Theology, Physical Education, History,

Geography, Life skills, Information Technology education and many others are very important and they enable individuals to achieve success.

When I later went to university to specialise in Journalism and Media Studies, I felt at home. I enjoyed the writing assignments and asking questions. I felt challenged. My lecturers asked us questions through which they expected us to analyse and be critical. There was a lot of reading to be done at university. We did group work, presentations and individual assignments. We carried out interviews and wrote news stories in business, politics and general social issues. The internship period was important as we got mentors. We were exposed to real life assignments. I remember being assigned to cover the First Lady then, and some prominent government officials in the first week of internship.

"Carolyne, you will go to an event at 2 in which the First Lady will be donating clothes to an orphanage," my editor, Mr. Bongani Ndlovu said. It was an instruction and I had to go there without fail. At first, nerves almost took the better part of me but I was quick to realise that I needed to be bold and do the assignment well because Mr. Ndlovu believed in me and I needed to show him that I could do the task. Thereafter, I did many assignments, attending council meetings, visiting rural communities, attending press conferences, cocktails and many other events. The internship was important for me to put theory into practice. It also provided opportunities for networking and to deepen my knowledge in journalism. Furthermore, it was important for me to showcase and sharpen my skills and abilities which would later become important in my career as a journalist and as a media educator.

I remember one classmate who was dismissed from the internship because of alcohol abuse. A very talented and hardworking individual who unfortunately spent his stipend on alcohol resulting in him missing work sometimes. Without completing the internship, he also could not progress into the final year. He therefore had to drop out. When I look back today, I realise that he lacked skills on how to manage his finances. Financial skills are important so that resources are distributed accordingly. How we use money is important and how much we have available for emergencies and uncertainties is also critical. Financial literacy skills are key to protecting one from debt and to be able to invest into today and the future and all young people need to have these skills so that they have a better today and tomorrow and fulfil their dreams.

Before I landed my first full time job in 2012, I had sent in hundreds of applications online. I rushed to send many applications within a short space of time. I was called to only three interviews and I did not make it. But the more I read about applying and more especially about online applications, I began to understand that online applications are very competitive and the people who usually make it are those who produce winning CVs and cover letters among other reasons. Their CVs are tailor-made to suit the jobs on offer, are not rushed and are free of errors among other factors. I stayed for 3 years at my first job and resigned when I felt that I needed a new challenge.

"You have made a bad decision," "how will you survive?" these are the comments that friends and relatives uttered to me daily. I was very fortunate because I immediately got into a university teaching contract which expired after two years and I found myself without a job. I remember how people around me felt so much pity for me. "So you are officially unemployed" my relatives and friends repeatedly said. "How will you survive?"some asked. I hated these questions because I found them annoying and I did not require anyone's pity because I was not feeling pity for myself. I started a business which failed. I did not make any money from it, instead it took away all my savings. I lacked a business model and failed to get paying

6

customers. I did not have any mentors from whom I could learn from and I lacked knowledge in finance, accounting, marketing and the ability to sell successfully. My way of doing business was all wrong. I am in the process of starting one and learning from my mistakes.

I began the job application process again and took 3 part time jobs at the same time which kept me very busy. I also applied for scholarships to pursue a PhD overseas. I was offered a place but did not qualify for any scholarships. It was devastating but I did not lose hope. The part time jobs were important because I remained relevant, networked, acquired experience and got money for survival. But most important of all, I was very positive about my future. I did not allow negativity to engulf me. I applied for opportunities consistently and thoroughly. I believed that God would give me what was due to me at the right time. I spoke to people, checked online platforms until I was offered my current job after a successful online application.

As I continue to live, I have become acutely aware of the importance of young people to think about their past, present and future lives. More importantly in this complex environment we live in. The advancements in technology, the rise of social media and how it impacts our lives everyday is something to think about very seriously. It is important for young people to be aware of who they are who and most importantly who they are becoming. It is important for young people to keep up to date with media but to do so with criticality. They need to sift information and engage in positive habits when online. Young people should always think about the things that they can do in order to be successful and not engage in destructive habits. Addiction to platforms such as WhatsApp and Facebook are detrimental to one's health. Spending long hours looking at statuses and profiles can cause depression and bring psychological problems in future and shows lack of time management and inability to set and fulfil one's goals. Abusing alcohol and drugs do not bring success. They are recipes for disaster. Having multiple sexual partners is a sign that one does not care about his/her health and the health of the other people. They also do not care about their future. Living healthy lives is determined by what we take into our bodies. Alcohol and drug abuse do not bring a healthy life. Instead, they eat the body away, eat one's wealth and alienates them from their loved ones. Successful young people are self aware. They are conscious of their health, well being and engage in exercise. Managing stress is also important. Tolerance and being able to live well with others enables one to avoid conflict.

If you have continued to read until here, you by now may have an idea of what this book is about. This book has been written to provide in-depth information on the critical skills that are important for successful youths. The world is changing rapidly. We live in a globalised world in which information, the internet, and social media are at the centre of what we do. Socially, economically and politically we are witnessing change. As changes continue to intensify, the more uncertain, confusing and challenging the world is becoming for youths. High unemployment rates, increasing poverty levels, shrinking economies, poor service delivery, loss of hope, diseases such as HIV/AIDS are some of the problems youths are confronted with daily.

This book seeks to revive hope among young people in high school, at tertiary level, in employment and those in business, by offering a practical guide on how to overcome daily challenges and thrive in today's digitalised and globalised world. The book identifies and describes the essential/critical skills which put youths on the path to success. It goes on to give real life examples and provide steps which young people should follow in order to be successful.

21st Century Skills is a term dominating discussions about what makes an effective educational experience. Competencies such as problem-solving, critical thinking and teamwork are listed among the 21st-century skills or global life skills and their importance to all young people cannot be overemphasised. They may be defined through many lenses, but whatever the lens may be, the discussion on essential or critical skills centres on the development of personal learning outcomes that provide a foundation for success beyond the academic experience.

Skills identified in the book include lifelong learning, critical thinking, problem solving, entrepreneurship, financial literacy, creativity and innovation, emotional intelligence, Information and Communication Technology (ICT) skills which include social media skills among others. Lifelong learning calls on youths to continue learning not only in the programme of their study but throughout their lives. This they can do by taking advantage of online courses so as to broaden their skills and remain relevant in their chosen fields.

Critical thinking requires that youths not take things and information at face value but break them into smaller components in order to get to their deeper meaning. The asking of questions such as why and what, is important for getting at the bottom of an issue. Problem solving skills call on youths to be able to handle difficult and unexpected situations in their personal lives, at school and at the workplace, provide solutions and take the necessary action which will result in happiness.

Entrepreneurship skills challenge youths to start businesses by solving problems that affect people in their daily lives. Through businesses, youths can create more employment, fight poverty, contribute to the economy and live successful and fulfilling lives. Financial literacy requires that youths know how to create wealth and embark on saving strategies at an early age. Selling, seeking opportunities, dealing with fear and doubt in business are of paramount importance if youths want to become financially independent.

By being creative and innovative, youths can generate new ideas through exploring new possibilities and bring those ideas into reality. In order to be highly successful, youths should harness the power of emotional intelligence so as to manage their own emotions and those of others as this is useful in guiding one's thinking and the necessary actions to take. Positive thinking is a challenge I pose to youths so that they believe in themselves and do away with negative thoughts, which can come from their own thinking, friends, parents or co-workers as this is detrimental to success.

SECTION ONE-THINKING SKILLS

Chapter 1

Critical Thinking

1.1   What is Critical Thinking?

The 21st Century requires young people who are critical thinkers. According to Paul and Elder (2014), critical thinking is the art of using the best thinking one is capable of in any circumstance which results in good choices. In other words, it is using the mind to make sense of information (Cottrell 2017). In addition, clear and rational thinking about what to do constitute critical thinking. This also encompasses reflection and the ability to think independently. Critical thinking "as a skill refers to the ability to assess the value of a claim or information and come to a conclusion about what to believe or to do about it" (Lamb et al 2017: 19).

Do not be confused as critical thinking is sometimes called analytical thinking or creative thinking. Paul and Elder (2014: 9) say that good thinking pays off while poor thinking causes problems and mistakes you will later regret. Nomatter the programme you are studying, Computer Science, Law, Social work, Journalism, Education, Theology, Biology, Engineering, Accounting and Finance, History, Agriculture among others, you should demonstrate the ability to think critically because these skills are important in all fields. This means not taking situations, people, ideas or things at face value. Critical thinking requires you to analyse arguments beyond the surface. By this we mean digging deeper to find hidden meanings. You should be able to question, probe and identify the importance of ideas and how you can apply them in your life.

1.2   How to Develop Critical Thinking Skills?

There are a variety of ways for you to develop critical thinking skills. Some of the ways include:
- Talking to others so that you learn how others think and what influences their thinking thus enabling you to appreciate diverse viewpoints.
- Knowing your subject/area of specialisation very well.
- Engaging in debates makes you to think deeper in order to come up with convincing arguments and analyse an issue fully.
- Questioning your biases so as to avoid taking situations and things for granted
- Questioning intensely (what is going on, are they trying to take advantage of me, why has this information been said this way etc.)
- Reading a lot, i.e. books, novels, magazines and newspapers and asking what, why and how things have happened.
- Listening to how other people argue and make strong arguments
- Listening to elderly advice if it is sound

1.3   Why Critical Thinking Skills are Important?

Africa and the world at large are plagued with problems; poverty, rising cases of abuse etc. Individuals who possess critical thinking skills can use available information to find solutions to these problems. For example, how can a family deal with the problem of poverty? The first thing would be for that family to see that poverty is a problem and that they would need to come up with practical strategies to overcome it.   There are ways that they can deal with poverty in the short and also in the long term. In the short term, the family can set up a small business and generate income through it. In the long term, the family would need to encourage their children to get an education, learn about entrepreneurship, start a business, create employment and make a life that is free from poverty etc. This is done through questioning, researching, implementation and evaluation which are key in critical thinking. In some African countries such as South Africa and Eswatini among others, community members have established savings groups or stokvels and these can be used to break poverty in families if the money is invested or used to start projects. You should take heed to such and start saving little by little, invest and start life-changing projects. Give yourself time to study these stokvels and your surroundings, evaluate what works and what does not and develop a unique project.

In the fast changing world of the internet, critical thinking skills are important so that you analyse information coming from diverse sources and be able to solve problems. Karshner (2014) says that critical thinking helps one make a positive contribution to a debate after scrutinising ideas and facts. Being open minded about life is also important to critical thinkers.

1.4 Questions Critical Thinkers ask
When you possess critical thinking skills, you should ask questions as listed below:

- Why is there is an increase in A?
- How do I reduce the rise in A?
- What aspects of my culture need to be changed and why?
- What values should I promote to eradicate B etc?
- Why is this happening in this way?
- What is missing here?
- Whose side is fore-grounded and why and vice versa?
- How else can this story be told?

1.5 Asking these questions will enable us to:

- Build a better tomorrow

- Protect innocent and vulnerable groups such as children.
- Promote love in the family and community.
- Do away with practices that are harmful and dangerous.
- Promote a better world which is devoid of problems.

As a young person, you should be able to think freely and broadly. We are used to the saying that one should think outside the box. Young people should think as if there was no box/without limit or they should think in other terms and be not restricted by anything.

1.6   What do Critical Thinkers do?

Based on Scheffer and Rubenfeld (2001), critical thinking youths should:

Analyse (Breakdown information into small components)	*Apply Standards* (Judging something according to a certain criteria)	*Seek information* (Study/Seek data)
Reason Logically (Drawing conclusions that are supported with examples)	*Predict* (Forecasting/Envisioning the outcome)	*Transform knowledge* (Improving)

In the 21st Century, critical thinking skills are of paramount importance. We are living in an era of fake news and disinformation which call on all individuals to be vigilant when it comes to accessing information, making sense of it and taking important decisions. Critical thinking skills will ensure that we do not take for granted what we consume but instead take it more seriously and ask important questions (who, what, when, why, how etc.). As shown in the above diagram, we should analyse information we get from the media so that we arrive at the truth.

References

1. Cottrell, S. 2017. Critical Thinking Skills: Effective Analysis, Argument and Reflection. London: Macmillan International Higher Education.
2. Karshner, D.L. 2013. Be a Critical Thinker: Hone Your Mind to think critically. Bullen.https://www.amazon.com/Be-Critical-Thinker-Think-Critically/dp/0615783740Accessed 15 March 2019.
3. Lamb, S. Maire, Q. and Doecke, E. 2017. Key Skills of the 21st Century: an evidence based review https://education.nsw.gov.au/our-priorities/innovate-for-the-future/education-for-a-changing-world/research-findings/future-frontiers-analytical-report-key-skills-for-the-21st-century/Key-Skills-for-the-21st-Century-Analytical-Report.pdf Accessed 16 March 2019.
4. Paul, R. And Elder, L. 2014. Critical thinking skills for taking charge of your professional and personal
5. Scheffer, B.K. and Rubenfield, M. G. 2001. Critical Thinking: What is it and how do we teach? Current issues in Nursing. umich.edu/☐essen/html/probsolv/strategy/ctskills.htm
6. Schuster, S. 2018. The Critical Thinker: The Path to Better Problem Solving, Accurate Decision Making, and Self-Disciplined Thinking. Create Space Independent Publishing Platform.
7. What is Critical Thinking? https://philosophy.hku.hk/think/critical/ct.php

Accessed 23 March 2019

8. Wilson, S. 2018. New Critical Thinking.What Wittgenstein Offered. London: Rowman and Littlefield.

Chapter 2

Problem Solving

2. What is a Problem?

We encounter problems in our lives every day. According to the Business Dictionary, a problem is a gap between the existing and the desired state. Problems are unwelcome and need to be overcome in order to restore the status quo. You should be able to solve problems of whatever nature which you may encounter at the workplace, college or at home. The idea of problem solving should not appear like an abstract thing because we come across problems everyday and also come up with solutions and take action. Personal problems should not interfere with work or your education as problems are never permanent. It is important for you to deal with personal issues so as to be more focused at work or at school or in a project that you are embarking on.

2.1 Problems individuals face everyday

- Missing the bus to school
- Two tests on the same day
- Missing a test due to transport delays
- Power outage while cooking
- Late because alarm did not go off
- No lunch money

Businesses also face problems all the time. They may encounter hard to deal with customers and machine breakdowns. According to Robertson (2001) problem solving skills at the workplace include the ability to handle difficult or unexpected situations. As a young person, you should be able to respond positively to problems. Problem solving skills cut across careers and different people

18

encounter them in their work daily. Teachers encounter problems when they are dealing with learners and other teachers. Doctors also face problems with patients not disclosing all the necessary information to ensure a proper diagnosis and sometimes shortage of drugs. Pharmacists face problems when there are unable to provide certain drugs. To solve these problems, a range of other skills are important which go together with problem solving skills as will be discussed in the chapter.

2.2   How Problems Arise?

Dunker (1945:1) in Robertson (2001: 2) says a problem arises

> "when a living creature has a goal but does not know how this goal is to be reached. Whenever one cannot go from the given situation to the desired situation simply by action, then there is recourse to thinking....Such thinking has the task of devising some action which may mediate between the existing and the desired situation".

Examples of problems (1 and 2)

(Given situation)	**BLOCK** (Problem)	(Desired situation)
1 Me at home 2. Me unemployed	**1. Long distance** 2. Lack of capital	**1. Me at university** 2. Me running a business

Robertson (2001) notes that if you know what action is to be taken then it is not a problem. If you do not then you have a problem. You will have to take action that will lead you to the desired outcome. In the above diagram, you have to find the solution to overcome the problem and move from home and get to the university (for example 1). You may have to walk or find transport that will take you there. For example 2, for you to solve the problem of unemployment, you will need to find capital and start a business. It requires you to take action, meet people, talk about what you desire until you get it among other strategies.

2.3   Skills that go together with Problem Solving?

See: www.indeed.com/career-advice/resumes-cover-letters/problem-solving-skills

20

From the skills listed above, we will demonstrate how some of them are important in the process of solving problems.

Research

Research is very important to get to the bottom of a problem. You need to consult a variety of materials for you to understand where the problem is emanating from. Colleagues who are more experienced, articles online or in libraries are good sources of information.

Analysis

In order to understand a problem you need to be able to analyse it. By analysing information, we mean putting something under thorough scrutiny, or carefully studying it. You may also break it down into small parts so as to get a full understanding of how each small part contributes to the problem.

Decision Making

Decision making is critical when it comes to searching for solutions. There are some people who cannot make decisions or provide solutions to problems. Some youths, when faced with problems, sit and fold their hands and wait for a miracle to happen. They say that the problem will solve itself. No problem ever solved itself. When you get into a situation, carefully examine it, and then act firmly to solve it. There are persistent problems in our society because young people do not want to use their brains to think about possible solutions. You need to do away with such habits.

Communication

Communication is very important in the workplace, school and in business, when it comes to solving problems. You will need to communicate with colleagues, your superior or fellow classmates regarding the problem and how to solve it. Clear communication is important for avoiding confusion and misunderstanding. There are some youths who are unable to communicate while others fear expressing themselves to colleagues or their superiors. It is important to follow set procedures when communicating a problem. Not following communication policies in an institution can have detrimental results. If you have not been oriented on what the proper communication channels are at your workplace, school or college, you have to seek information from your immediate supervisor, lecturer or from the counselling officer.

Dependability

Being dependable is key when it comes to problem solving. As a dependable colleague, you do what is expected of you in a timely manner. Meeting deadlines for when specific problems should be solved, in a company, personal business or in the family is important. If time is not enough, it is important to communicate with your superior or lecturer and ask for more time. Lack of communication affects trust and results in loss of faith in people who are unable to solve problems and do not communicate on the progress of what they have done.

2.4   Solving problems

Runco (1994) and Mackall (2004) note that there are a number of strategies you should employ in order to solve problems:

- **Research**

This involves finding out how others who have faced a similar problem have dealt with it.

- **Being well versed with the technical knowledge of one's field**

There is no justification for you not performing duties that relate to what you have studied. It is thus important to have in depth knowledge about your field in order to be efficient. Technical skills are becoming more and more important in the world of work. Employees have to perform tasks fully and guide those who are under their supervision. If you know that there are some skills that you need to stay on top of your game, take online courses, seek internships and find mentors. Always challenge yourself to continue learning so that you acquire those skills.

- **Learning from more experienced colleagues**

You should always humble yourself so that you learn from more experienced professionals. It does not matter that these people have lower educational qualifications. If they have been in a job for many years, it means that they are more experienced and you can learn a lot from their expertise (mentorship). This may also include always asking questions and observing how they solve problems. After formulating a solution, it is important to develop a plan of action to implement the solution.

Solving Problems

Engel (1998) notes that problem solving can be learned by solving problems. Some individuals are afraid of solving problems as they fear making mistakes. You should not be afraid of taking calculated risks. The experience of solving problems makes you become better at it. For example, if you are in a sales position and a customer approaches you with a problem do not say "that is not my responsibility" or say "do not ask me" or refer that person to someone else. Take the necessary action and help that person. Referring the person to someone else will portray you negatively unless if the issue is not in your line of duty or is beyond what you can do.

As we continue to live, we will continue to encounter problems. It is important that we respond positively to problems so as to carry on with our lives. Problem solving skills are important at home, school, in business and in the workplace.

References

1.   Engel, A. 1998. Problem Solving Strategies. New York: Springer.
2.   Mackall, D.D. 2004. Problem Solving. Ferguson: New York.
3.   Robertson, I. S. 2001. Problem Solving. Taylor and Francis: Philadelphia.
4.   Runco, M. A. (ed) 1994. Problem Solving and Creativity. Alex publishing: New Jersey.
5.   Toll, A.C. 2018. Educational Coaching: A Partnership for Problem Solving. Virginia: ASCD
6.   Van Aken, J. E. Berends, H. 2018. Problem Solving in Organisations. Cambridge: Cambridge University Press

Chapter 3

Creativity and Innovation

3.   What is Creativity?

Creativity is defined as the ability to make new conceptions between old ideas. Maria Popova of Brainpickings defines it as "our ability to tap into our 'inner' pool of resources – knowledge, insight, information, inspiration and all the fragments populating our minds – that we've accumulated over the years just by being present and alive and awake to the world and to combine them in extraordinary new ways." There is no agreed-upon definition of creativity that most researchers use, even though most argue that it entails the production of something recognised as novel or useful in a given social context (Plucker et al., 2004).

Creativity is often associated with critical thinking in discussions on skills. You have the potential to be creative as long as you give yourself time to create something nomatter how poor or bad it turns out to be. Creativity is not only about writers, painters, music artists, singers or dancers. For writers to come up with creative pieces of writing, they have to write a lot. They may write a page and only discover that there is only one sentence that is written creatively. If they continue to write and share their work with others and get feedback, they will improve, continue to write and rewrite etc. That is the process you have to prepare yourself for in order to develop your creative capacity. According to United Nations Educational, Scientific and Cultural Organisation (UNESCO), creativity involves creating, learning and experimenting. This means that creativity comes from making mistakes through doing. As emphasised earlier, doing more will lead to creativity. To be creative, you should not be afraid of failing. Instead you should keep going until you get it right.

Being consistent is also important for creativity. You may not come up with something amazing at first but continuously working on it will lead you towards something out of the ordinary. There are some people who do not accomplish anything because they do not start or do anything. They keep procrastinating until they are discouraged to even do anything. Being creative does not come to lazy people. It requires people who are hardworking and focused. It is a process requiring you to overcome stumbling blocks and allowing your creative genius to blossom. Developing positive thinking is also critical for creativity as it enables you to keep trying while believing that something good will come out of it. Stress, depression and lack of happiness can cause you to fail to think creatively. Nomatter the craft you are in, give yourself time think creatively.

3.1   What is Innovation?

The Business Dictionary defines innovation as "the process of translating an idea or invention into a good service that creates value for which customers will pay. To be called an innovation, an idea has to satisfy the needs and expectations of the customers". Skills that are associated with innovation include taking initiative, risk taking, communication and imagination. Hardwork, collaboration and leadership skills are also important for bringing innovation.

3.2   The Relationship between Creativity and Innovation

Innovation is a result of creativity. Creativity is thinking of something new while innovation is the implementation of something new (Paulus et al 2003). Associate Professor of Management at Oral Roberts University, David Burkus, says innovation is the application of ideas that are novel and useful while creativity is the ability to generate novel and useful ideas. Innovation is thus great ideas (creativity) executed brilliantly to solve a problem. There are a number of ways of fostering innovation through creativity as suggested by different scholars. For example, work places should create a stimulating environment which allows for free flow of ideas among employees. Management should encourage employees to take calculated risks and invest time, people or money in order to prototype innovative ideas (Business Dictionary). Innovative products display new features which allow users to have a better experience. The Royal Science and Technology Park (RSTP) in Eswatini created through the vision of His Majesty, King Mswati 111, promotes science, technology and innovation to start ups with the aim of nurturing entrepreneurship. There are many other innovation hubs across Africa and the world at large which provide individuals with platforms to collaborate and develop innovative products.

3.3   Importance of Creativity

- Allows one to gain cognitive skills, scientific method, dexterity and exertion, problem solving and the ability to identify symbols, patterns and shapes.
- Allows for self-expression.
- Allows for the development of coping mechanisms.

- Provides others with a way to learn more about what the child may be thinking or feeling.
- Promotes mental growth by providing opportunities for experimenting with new ideas, new ways of thinking and problem-solving.
- Helps acknowledge and celebrates the uniqueness of personalities and diversity

Source: https://paisleypark.com.au/importance-creativity-2/

3.4 The Creativity process

Gather new material

During this stage you focus on learning specific material directly related to your task and learning general material by becoming fascinated with a wide range of concepts.

Thoroughly work over the materials in your mind

During this stage, you examine what you have learned by looking at the facts from different angles and experimenting with fitting various ideas together.

Step away from the problem

Next, you put the problem completely out of your mind and go do something else that excites you and energizes you.

Let your idea return to you

At some point, but only after you have stopped thinking about it, your idea will come back to you with a flash of insight and renewed energy.

Shape and develop your idea based on feedback.

You will then go back to your idea and develop it further by incorporating feedback

Source: Creativity: How to Unlock Your Hidden Creative Genius
https://jamesclear.com/creativity

30

3.5   Becoming Innovative

Innovation is the process that follows after creativity. It requires you to:
1. Have an idea (s)
2. Invest time and money
3. Attend innovation trainings and workshops
4. Turn ideas into new products/ execute the idea
5. Address a real challenge
6. Address a new market

3.6   Skills Innovative People Display

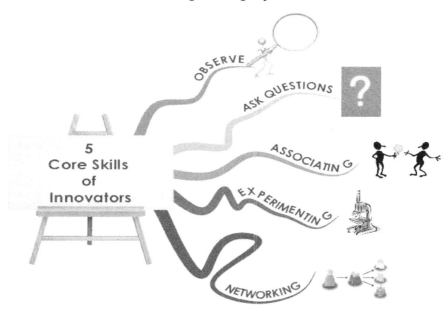

Source: http://www.engagevisually.co.uk/tag/network/
(Picture colour altered)

3.7   Creativity, Innovation and the Knowledge Economy

Creativity and innovation are important in the 21st Century. You should formulate an idea, research about it, implement the idea and bring forth something new. It does not matter what background you have. You may be from a previously disadvantaged background and still be in school or college. You should challenge the status quo and come up with something new and in the knowledge economy, listening to customers is very important. The internet provides businesses with opportunities to interact with their customers. That way they get feedback instantly which can be used to improve existing products or come with new ones. You can enhance your creativity by collaborating, researching and doing experiments. New thinking can bring about a positive change, and help you fully unleash your potential and make the best of your life. Always give yourself enough time to think. Research as possible.

References

1. Clear, J.Creativity is a process not an event. https://jamesclear.com/creative-thinkingAccessed 24 December 2018.

2. Greenwald, M. 2014. What exactly is innovation? https://www.forbes.com/sites/michellegreenwald/2014/03/12/what-exactly-is-innovation/#613b7f175e5a 12 March 2014. Accessed 21 January 2019.

3. Kim, K. H. 2011. The Creativity Crisis: The Decrease in Creative Thinking Scores on the Torrance Tests of Creative Thinking. Creativity Research Journal, Volume 23, Issue 4, 2011.

4. Youth and Creativity https://en.unesco.org/creativity/node/582Accessed 16 November 2018.

5. Plucker, J. A. 2005. The (Relatively) Generalist View of Creativity. In J.C. Kaufman and J. Baer (eds), Creativity Across Domains: Faces of the Muse (pp 307-312). Mahwah. Lawrence Erlbaum.

6. Recke, M. 2019. What is Innovation?https://nextconf.eu/2019/02/what-is-innovation/#grefAccessed 15 February 2019.

7. Experts Share Innovation Definition. https://www.ideatovalue.com/inno/nickskillicorn/2016/03/innovation-15-experts-share-innovation-definition/Accessed 12 January 2019.

8. What is Creativity?https://www.creativityatwork.com/2014/02/17/what-is-creativity/Accessed 15 January 2019.

9. Paulus, P. B. and Nijstad, B. A. 2003. Group Creativity: Innovation through Collaboration Oxford University Press.
10. There's A Critical Difference Between Creativity And Innovationhttps://www.businessinsider.com/difference-between-creativity-and-innovation-2013-4 10 April 2013

Chapter 4

Emotional Intelligence

4.   What is Emotional Intelligence?

Emotional intelligence is referred to as the ability to manage one's emotions as well as those of others. Zeidner et al (2004) adds that this enables one to guide one's thinking and actions. Individuals should be able to regulate their emotions when necessary and be able to calm or cheer up others. Emotional intelligence is on the list of key skills employers are looking for nowadays and is sometimes referred to as emotional quotient. Cooper (1997) in Zeidner et al (2004) notes that people with high levels of emotional intelligence succeed at communicating their ideas, goals and intentions than those without. Such people are more successful in their careers, build stronger personal relationships, lead more effectively and enjoy better health than those with low emotional intelligence. They are able to deal with stress in a calm manner. Leaders with high emotional intelligence generate excitement, enthusiasm and optimism among employees and build quality interpersonal relations than those without (Zeidner et al 2004).

4.1   How to use Emotional Intelligence in the Workplace

Emotional intelligence can be used in the workplace to bring positive results. With high emotional intelligence skills you will be able to:
- Improve awareness about yourself
- Remain calm under pressure
- Remain motivated

- Improve self regulation
- Show empathy
- Improve social skills
- Resolve conflicts

Below is an elaboration of some of the points we have identified above.

- **Improving one's self-awareness**

You should pay attention to how you are feeling throughout your day and noticing how your emotions contribute to your decisions and actions as they regulate your behavior towards others including what you say to them. In addition, you should identify and understand your emotional strengths and weaknesses and understand that emotions can be fleeting and easily changed.

- **Practicing self-regulation**

Finding techniques that help you deal with work-related stress, like hobbies, exercise, meditation, etc. is of great importance in overcoming stressful situations.

There are moments at school or work when the work gets crazy. It is something that happens to everyone. You should try to accept reality and remain calm and always give yourself time to think and plan before making decisions especially big ones. Do not shout or get angry at the next person when you are under pressure. You are better off doing the work and remaining silent. The same should apply when co-workers are experiencing pressure and they take it out on you.

- **Improving your social skills**

Listening actively and attentively to your managers, co-workers, and peers is important in the workplace and at school so that you minimise misunderstandings. During the communication process, always keep an eye out for non-verbal communication (gestures, facial expressions etc) because actions speak louder than words. Be sure to handle conflict wisely when appropriate and necessary.

- **Becoming more empathetic**

Strive to always put yourself in other people's shoes at work and in your personal life. This will make you understand other people much better. Always think first before you respond to someone and pay attention to your own responses to others so that you avoid hateful language which will later cause regret.

- **Working on your motivation**

Focus on what you love about your job/programme of study rather than what you hate about it. This will ensure that you maintain a positive and optimistic attitude and succeed in all your tasks (Cherry 2018).

Source: https://positivepsychologyprogram.com/emotional-intelligence-workplace/

4.2   Facts about Emotional Intelligence
- A lot of the times co-workers or class mates may criticise you. It is important that you do not become angry and fight.
- Contain your emotions and not be irritated easily during stressful times.
- Not hurting the feelings of others is important for building successful relationships.
- It is important to treat others with respect and kindness.
- Act professionally at all times.
- Practice active listening and understand what is being communicated before you respond.
- The Golden Rule, treat others the way you want to be treated is of paramount importance and links with self awareness. It

applies to how we treat colleagues in lower or higher positions and fellow classmates if it is in a school situation.

"Harnessing the power of emotional intelligence at work and home is no longer a choice. In order to succeed, you must master these skills," (Bradberry and Greaves 2006). Engaging in petty arguments and debate and wanting to come out as a winner is inappropriate and shows lack of emotional intelligence skills. It is also crucial to understand other people's personalities, cultural orientation, and position in the company in order to improve relationships with them. Introspection or looking inwardly is an important aspect of improving emotional intelligence. It is important for you to recognise your own thought processes, emotions, and biases and regulating yourself accordingly. Introspection brings about such recognition.

4.3   Low vs High Emotionally Intelligent People

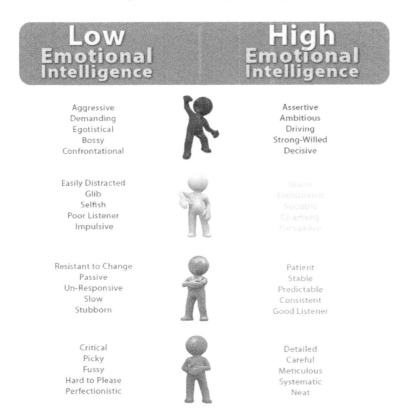

Source: https://www.pinterest.com/pin/132363676525938747/
(Picture colour altered)

High emotionally intelligent individuals are careful and pay close attention to their environment so as to respond appropriately. In order to be successful at what you do you should have high emotional intelligence.

References

1. Bradberry, T. Are You Emotionally Intelligent? Here's How to Know for Sure https://www.inc.com/travis-bradberry/are-you-emotionally-intelligent-here-s-how-to-know-for-sure.htmlAccessed 12 January 2019.

2. Bradberry, T. and Greaves, J. 2006. The Emotional Intelligence Quick Book: Everything You Need to Know to Put Your EQ to Work.Simon and Schuster.

3. Emotional Intelligence in the workplace. https://liveboldandbloom.com/02/self-awareness-2/emotional-intelligence-workplaceAccessed 12 January 2019.

4. Emotional Intelligence in the Workplace: A Key to Communication https://appliedpsychologydegree.usc.edu/blog/emotional-intelligence-in-the-workplace/Accessed 16 January 2019

5. Gardner, H. (1983). *Frames of mind: The theory of multiple intelligences*. New York: Basic Books.

6. Emotional Intelligence. www.psychologytoday.com/us/basics/emotional intelligence/Accessed 12 January 2019.

7. Zeidner, M. Matthews, G. Roberts, R.D. 2004. Emotional Intelligence in the workplace: A critical review. Applied Psychology: An international review, 53 (3) 371-399.

Chapter 5

Decision Making

5.   What is Decision Making?

The Dartmouth University defines decision making as the process of making choices by identifying a decision, gathering information and assessing the alternative resolutions. Bolland and Lopes (2018) say it is setting goals and specifying the course of action. Making thoughtful decisions is important for all individuals. The ability to realise which alternatives you have, and also consider the benefits and disadvantages before making the final decision is an important skill. Decision making is an important function of leaders or managers and it links with other skills such as critical thinking (Bakke 2013). We make decisions in our lives everyday on basic things; decisions about what to cook, what to wear, whether to go to a seminar, enrolling at a college or taking an online course. Some decisions are easy while others are complex and can be stressful. Decision making may require you to consider time, cost, impact/results. There are no shortcuts to decision making, instead they can be costly and bring disastrous results.

You will notice that where you had to make decisions there were other competing alternatives which you had to evaluate and take the one with the best possible outcome. As a student, when it is raining and you are used to walking to school, you have to consider what options you have; walking and getting wet, borrowing an umbrella or catching the bus. The three options have their own strengths and weaknesses. Weighing them and considering the best one, i.e. the one with the best outcome is what we call decision making. Failing to decide might lead you to failing to go to school and missing out on the work scheduled for that day.

According to the United Nations International Children's Emergency Fund (UNICEF)children, including adolescents, must be allowed to exercise their right to express their own views freely in accordance with their evolving capacity. They must be enabled to acquire knowledge and skills, such as for conflict resolution, communication and decision-making (https://www.unicef.org/violencestudy/pdf/call_action.pdf).

Their rights to express themselves must be respected and promoted and their views considered. The Convention on the Rights of the Child (CRC), the World Programme of Action for Youth to the Year 2000 and Beyond (WPAY), the World Fit for Children (WFFC), the United Nations Millennium Declaration and other international instruments and treaties all clearly state that children and young people have the right to participate in public life.

In various contexts around the world, children are not considered in decision making because they are considered of a lower social status than adults. Meanwhile, girls are not given the same opportunities as boys due to existing attitudes in which girls are considered inferior to boys. According to UNICEF, education systems often fail to prepare young people adequately to participate in decision-making. They do not develop the necessary analytical skills for critical thinking or problem solving through participatory and active learning. Being equipped with decision making skills is important as you will continue making decisions throughout your life.

5.1   The Importance of Decision Making

- **Planning and developing policies**

Without decision making, no policies or plans can be made. In the process of making plans, appropriate decisions must be made after considering a variety of alternatives.

- **Selecting the best alternatives**

Decision makers select the best alternatives from negatives and positives (Bolland and Lopes 2018). Good decision makers evaluate the advantages and disadvantages of various alternatives or options before they select on the best one.

- **Brings about success**

Successful organisations are built on effective decision making. In this highly competitive era, organisations can only thrive if the best decisions have been made. In schools, successful students are those who make good decisions about what to study and how to study, including decisions about where to seek information.

- **Helps evaluate performance**

Successful and effective leaders make good decisions. It is through decisions that leaders can be judged. When the outcomes are good it means the leader came up with a good decision and vice versa.

- **Enables businesses/organisations to function**

No organisation can function if decisions are not taken. Similarly, for youths to be able to enrol at college or university, they have to first make a decision. Nothing in this life happens without decision making. But good decision making is important.

- **Preventing chaos**

Failure to make decisions can result in chaos, especially where there is an imminent threat of a strike, danger or a disastrous situation. Effective leaders detect the smoke before the fire breaks out and act timeously.

5.2 The Importance of Youth Participation in Decision Making Processes:

- Leads to better decisions and outcomes.

- Is an integral part of a democratic society.
- Strengthens young people's understanding of human rights and democracy.
- Promotes social integration and cohesion in society.
- Encourages more young people to participate by example.

Source: https://www.unicef.org/violencestudy/pdf/call_action.pdf

5.3   Developing Decision Making Skills

For you to develop decision making skills you have to:
- Get training on decision making (At school these decisions come with solving problems, analysis and critical thinking skills).
- Find mentors and learn from how they make decisions
- Learn more on leadership and decision making from vast resources that are available online. Search and study information on decision making.
- Participate in leadership projects which will teach you on communicating with others. (In college you may take up positions in the Student Representative Council (SRC), societies, clubs and sports).

5.4   The Decision Making Process

The process of decision making is crucial and for this reason it should be done in a particular manner. Below is a diagram showing the steps involved.

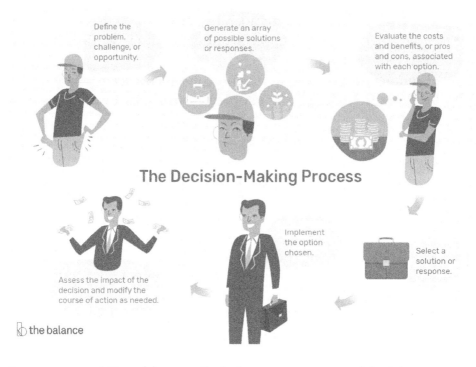

The Decision-Making Process

Define the problem, challenge, or opportunity.

Generate an array of possible solutions or responses.

Evaluate the costs and benefits, or pros and cons, associated with each option.

Assess the impact of the decision and modify the course of action as needed.

Implement the option chosen.

Select a solution or response.

the balance

Source: https://www.thebalancecareers.com/decision-making-skills-with-examples-2063748

Engaging in good decision making is crucial in avoiding problems in future. You should avoid bad decision making habits as they may lead you to failure and the creation of problems.

5.5   Bad Decision Making Habits

▪ **Not doing research**

Research on the benefits and disadvantages of a decision should be part of all decision making for you at school, college, home, work or in business. The amount of time invested in research should be in proportion with how big the decision to be made is. Potential costs, risks and outcomes should all be considered. Not doing research can result in negative consequences such as conflict, stress and loss of precious time.

- **Waiting too long**

Procrastination does not bring about good results. Instead opportunities may pass you if you fail to make decisions on time. But still, decisions should not be made instantly. As indicated earlier, it is wise to do the necessary research and then make a decision.

- **Wanting to please friends**

Decisions should not be made with the intention to please friends. As indicated earlier, proper considerations of possible risks, costs and outcomes should always be made if you are to make good decisions. Bad decision makers are not firm. They would rather sacrifice their own happiness because they want to appear good to friends. Some ask friends to help them decide because they themselves cannot take decisions and this can be detrimental.

- **Basing on instinct**

As indicated, proper research should be done before a proper decision is made. Do not promise what you cannot deliver by saying *"Ok I will try"*- when they know the task is difficult and they will not manage to do it. Be frank from the onset that you are unable to do the task at hand by saying, *"Sorry I do not think I can help you at this point in time"* or *"I am unable to do this"* or *"This is difficult for me"*.

Good decision making comes with experience. Do not be afraid to make decisions after doing research and considering the pros and cons so as to avoid negative consequences. Learn from how others make decisions and be firm with the decision you make. Be prepared to face the consequences.

References

1. Bakke, D. 2013.The Decision Maker: Unlock the Potential of Everyone in Your Organisation, One Decision at a Time. Pear: Washington.
2. Bolland, E. Jand Lopes, C. J. 2018. Decision Making and Business Performance. Cheltenham: Edward Elgar.
3. Children and Young People: Participating in Decision-Making https://www.unicef.org/violencestudy/pdf/call_action.pdf Accessed 12 November 2019
4. Decision-making process.https://www.umassd.edu/fycm/decision-making/process/ Accessed 15 January 2019.
5. Halpern-Felsher, B., Baker, M. and Stitzel, S. 2016. Decision making in adolescents and young adults. Handbook of Health Decision Science 157-167.
6. Shogren, K. A., Wehmeyer, M.L., Martinis, J. Blanck, P. 2018. Supported Decision-Making: Theory, Research, and Practice to Enhance Self-Determination and Quality of Life Cambridge: Cambridge University Press: Cambridge.

SECTION TWO:
ACTION/CREATIVITY
SKILLS

Chapter 6

Communication

6.   What is Communication?

Communication refers to the act of sending and receiving messages by way of speaking, writing or using media. Everyday we engage in a process of communication, verbally or non-verbally and we often take for granted how with communicate with other people (Arredondo 2000). Some people are unable to communicate while others do not think much about the communication process (ie. thinking carefully about what to communicate, communicating the message, receiving feedback etc). The communication process can be ongoing, one way, two way or multi-way and it is done for various reasons (sharing information, passing a message or expressing your feelings). Communication can sometimes be accidental, especially when one considers how with non-verbal communication you can send a message without the intention to do so. For example, wearing a certain kind of dress might be taken to mean what is not intended. How a message is encoded influences how it will be received.

Businesses also engage in communication everyday. According to Wrench (2013), different stakeholders require different communication strategies and for effective communication to take place in organisations all employees and management should be involved. They may engage in communication with customers, government or other businesses. Due to the influence of globalisation, communicators need to think of how to communicate in a global context, in a professional, effective and successful manner.

6.1   Skills for Effective Communication

Communication skills are very important for workplace and college success. The ability to communicate well is an important skill that brings forth positive results. According to Wells (2018), communicating effectively makes you valuable, self-confident and increases your worth. Effective communication is the lifeblood of a successful business, family and relationship (ibid). In the workplace, communication can take place in meetings, with customers, between co-workers of the same culture or of a different one, between the manager and subordinates etc. At college, communication can occur among students, with the lecturer or other staff etc.

As a young person seeking to develop yourself, you must be a master when communicating in different situations or contexts (Wells 2018). As alluded to in the chapter on Life Long Learning, online courses cater for a variety of subjects. Communication courses are vast. For example *Alison.com* offers online courses such as *Persuasion and motivation, Business writing, Cross cultural communication* and *International business*. Below is a diagram showing some important communication skills you should possess.

Essential Communication Skills for Your Career

Source: https://www.thebalancecareers.com/communication-skills-list-2063779

6.2 The Importance of Communication in the Workplace

1. Improving customer service. Well informed employees about a product/service can pass the information to customers without difficulty.
2. To understand expectations. For employees to do their work accordingly, they have to know what is expected of them and this comes from communication.
3. Boost team work. Team work requires communication from the inception of a project up to its end, including the outcome as it enables them towards a shared goal.
4. Increase understanding of the company. Employees should have a full understanding of the company, its business model, values, structure and where employees fit in.
5. Keeping employees up to date. The media provides information and educates society on what is happening around the world and this enables them to make informed

decisions. Because of advancements in technology news are delivered directly into your inbox on your mobile phone or ipad. The same applies for information coming through the organisation's intranet.

6. Minimising confusion. If products and processes are well communicated, confusion is minimised.
7. Making employees feel valued. Regular communication with employees shows that they are valued in an organisation
8. Encouraging an open environment. When communication lines in an organisation are open and clear, employees feel comfortable in putting their ideas and suggestions forward.
9. Supporting change. When there is a change of management or a new policy has been introduced, it is important for communication to be made with employees as it will make them understand and be more accommodating of the change.
10. Driving engagement. Communication make employees feel valued, especially if they are informed of what is happening in an organisation and are also given a chance to give feedback.

Source: www.johnslyvester.co.uk/communications/the-top-10-reasons-to-communicate

6.3 Ensuring Successful Communication

There are a number of ways you can employ to ensure successful communication. By successful communication, we mean sending the intended message correctly and receiving feedback.

- Show respect- respect other people's time and space
- Display positive body language. Body language can mean different things to different people in various contexts. It is always important to understand the context you are in so that you give the most appropriate body language.
- Listen actively. Listening well and fully is important. You should not be distracted by using your phone or computer from what the next person is saying to you. I have seen individuals remaining glued to their phone or computer

screen when talking to others and you can see that they are not paying full attention.

- Get along with others
- Be willing to give feedback including commending those who have done well.
- Be willing to ask questions especially where clarity is being sought
- Understand email etiquette. Most communication today is done online. When responding to an email, break it up, be concise and use bullet points. Avoid using slang and be professional at all times.
- Remain open minded. Be open to new ideas and ways of doing tasks.

In the era of internet communication, it is important to use the correct medium for communicating and to remain professional at all times. Do not communicate using hateful or offensive language on emails or on social media platforms. There are many examples of professionals who lost their jobs because of what they said on Twitter or Facebook which was deemed hateful or offensive and tarnishing the image of the employer. When you are online, exercise care and think twice before making a post. Employers nowadays look at your social media profiles before making a decision about whether to call you for an interview or not. Your Facebook, Twitter and Linked In Profiles should contain professional posts and portray you in a good light.

6.4   Developing Communication and Interpersonal skills

There are a variety of ways for you to develop communication and interpersonal skills. If you are still at school, you can do part time work where you deal with other students eg being a student assistant during orientation or registration. You may also do part time work as a tutor or in the library and that will help you develop important communication and problem solving skills. Such a role will enable you to build relationships with others and know how to explain, convince, persuade, listen actively, understand needs and remain professional. Part time work will also provide you with the opportunity to do presentations or explain research to those without specialist knowledge. You might have already done or do presentations in college. They enable you to develop skills of explaining to other people while building your confidence to stand in front of others.

There are a variety of other opportunities at college for developing communication and interpersonal skills. These include being a course or hall representative, voluntary work, mentorship and group discussions.

http://careerweb.leeds.ac.uk/info/4/make_yourself_employable/2 02/employability_skills/5

6.5 Checklist for Good Communication

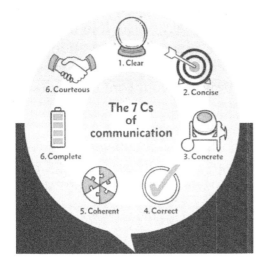

Source: https: //www.quora.com/What-are-examples-of-good-communication

References

1. Arredondo, L. 2000. Communicating Effectively. New York: McGraw Hill.
2. Goodall, H. L. Jr., Goodall, S. and Schiefelbein., J.2009. Business and Professional Communication in the Global Workplace. Wadsworth: Cengage.
3. Weisman, S. 2018. Overcoming The 7 Deadliest Communication SINs: A New Standard for Workplace Communication: Build a Championship Work Environment to Get Things Done and Make More Money. Auburn: Lynx Cat Press.
4. Wells, A. 2018. The Tech Professional's Guide to Communicating in a Global Workplace: Adapting Across Cultural and Gender Boundaries. Ohio: Apress.
5. Wrench, J. S (ed) 2013. Workplace Communication for the 21st Century: Tools and Strategies that Impact the Bottom Line [2 volumes]: Tools and Strategies That Impact the Bottom Line, Volume 1. Praeger: California.
6. 10 Steps to improve your workplace communication skills.https://www.thejobnetwork.com/10-steps-to-improve-your-workplace-communication-skills/Accessed 5 February 2019.
7. The power of good communication in the workplace. https://leadershipchoice.com/power-good-communication-workplace/Accessed 5 February 2019.
8. 7 Important workplace communication skills. https://www.fastcompany.com/90313078/the-importance-of-these-7-communication-skills Accessed 4 February 2019.
9. The Importance of good communication in the workplace. https://www.michaelpage.co.uk/advice/management-advice/development-and-retention/importance-good-communication-workplaceAccessed 4 February 2019.

Chapter 7

Media and Information Literacy

7.   What is Media and Information Literacy?

We are living in an era in which information drives everything that we do. The internet is awash with credible and less credible sources and it is up to all citizens to acquire competencies in media and information so that they make decisions based on true, verifiable and authentic information. Websites, blogs, databases, magazines, books, documentaries, newspapers, television shows, organisations, advertisements, and agencies are all sources of information which need to be approached with a critical lense.

The United Nations Educational, Scientific and Cultural Organisation (UNESCO) developed the term in 2007 and says that media literacy includes the ability to access information and the capacity to analyse, understand its underlying agenda and participate actively in its creation. Media and Information literacy according to UNESCO, is made up of skills, competencies, attitudes and practices. We are information literate if we are able to use various tools to narrow an internet search and to verify sources. You should take advantage of the vast information on UNESCO sites including taking online courses and taking part in workshops in order to be media and information literate.

Information these days comes instantly into our mobile phones. You should not be in a hurry to go through the information (it could be celebrity gossip, political and economic developments etc) that comes into your phone or tablet without establishing its veracity. It is important to ascertain which of the information is the most important including establishing where it is coming from or who generated it. Furthermore, the information has to be checked for credibility or believability, which is done by checking if the event did occur or not. This includes using fact-checking sites among other strategies. Checking for bias is also critical. You have to check whether the language is value-laden, the presence of stereotypes, the point of view from which the issue is told, sources cited etc. You will need to check sites which have similar information and compare how the story is told. In the process of reading, you also have to interrogate your own personal biases. This includes asking yourself questions such as the following; does my sex, religious beliefs, life experiences, age interfere with how I read and make sense of an article? Summarising information and media literacy, Hobbs (2010) says that it includes:

- Making responsible choices, accessing information and comprehending information and ideas
- Analysing messages in a variety of forms by identifying the author, purpose and point of view, and evaluating the quality and credibility of the content
- Creating content in a variety of forms, making use of language, images, sound, and new digital tools and technologies
- Reflecting on one's own conduct and communication behavior by applying ethical principles.
- Taking social action by working individually and collaboratively to share knowledge and solve problems in the family and workplace

7.1   Steps involved in Media Literacy

- **Accessing**

Accessing information is the ability to obtain information. Media and information literacy also means being able to find or obtain information from credible sources.

- **Analysing**

Analysing information means to examine information systematically, carefully or closely. In other words, when you get information you should be able to break it down into small components and understand what it means.

- **Understanding**

Understanding information is being able to think about information, read, to know when and why something happens the way it happens. When you get access to a news article on the internet, you should be able to do several things in order to get to what that information really means. Asking yourself who the source is, breaking that article down by asking the following questions; what is the story about; what are the people/sources in the story saying; is what they are saying believable; what is absent in the story; whose voices are missing, can it be verified or corroborated by other people? This will enable you to get at the bottom of the story. If you go through a story and you fail to understand what it means (after going through it several times), find someone else who can help you understand what it means. When writing assignments, you should review different information sources and note down why the articles or stories were written, from what perspective was it written, whether it is factual or an opinion, and if the facts given were accurate. Security and safe practices are also important in information literacy. You should know how to use the internet safely and also be in a position to protect your privacy. Be able to use a variety of sources without plagiarising. Direct quotes should be properly attributed.

Creating

You should create content in a variety of forms, making use of language, images, sound, and new digital tools and technologies. Below is a diagram showing the steps we have identified as important for information and media literacy.

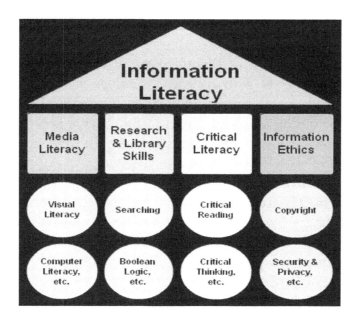

Source: https://www.pinterest.com/pin/63683782201732093/

7.2   Benefits of Media and Information Literacy

Information and media literacy skills have wide benefits in the digital era we are living in. The benefits include:

- Being able to apply for jobs online. You need skills to find relevant and credible information.
- Getting relevant health information. You need to be able to distinguish between good information for your health.
- Taking advantage of online educational opportunities. You need to have a good understanding of how knowledge is constructed, the reality it represents and the viewpoints that are fore-grounded and vice versa.

Source: Hobbs, R. 2010. Digital and Media Literacy: A Plan of Action.

7.3   Strategies of Detecting a Fake Site

We are living in an era of disinformation and fake news and it is important for you to know how to detect a fake site. Making decisions based on fake news may have detrimental consequences for you and your loved ones. Sharing fake news is also something you should avoid doing. Below are strategies for detecting one:

1. **Considering the source**
Mainstream media are more reliable because they verify their facts before reporting. Always look out for where information is coming from. Use Google to check who is behind that site etc.

2. **Examining the publisher's website closely**
Some of these sites openly admit that their stories are fiction or satire in the "About Us" section of the website (if they have one). Websites with .co at the end are not authentic. For example www.cnn.com.co

3. **Consulting the experts**
If something seems a little dodgy, as a reader, you can turn to a number of websites devoted exclusively to debunking fake news.

4. **Checking for quality**
Many fake news websites do not even try to do things properly, They will have punctuation, spelling, and grammar mistakes. Lacing headlines with words in all-capital letters is another favorite tactic of fake news writers. Their headlines insist that you "MUST READ" something. Do not read such websites

5. **Checking to see if anyone else is reporting the same thing**
Always check if other news sites carry the same story. It does not mean that if other news organisations have no covered it, it is false.

6. **Not stopping at the headline**
Reading the full story will enable you to ask critical questions. Headlines do not tell you everything that transpired so go beyond them.

7. **Scrolling down**

Comments by friends on social media platforms would indicate if information is true or false. Always check what others are saying about an issue.

Source: https://www.aarp.org/money/scams-fraud/info-2017/fake-news-alert-fd.html

7.4 Fact Checking Sites (some examples)

Name	Role
Snopes.com	Fights misinformation by providing a platform for fact checking
FactCheck.org	Monitors the factual accuracy of what is said by major United States (U.S.) political players in the form of television ads, debates, speeches, interviews and news releases.

There are more fact checking sites you can use. Ask experts if you are not sure. Information and media literacy skills are of paramount importance as they enable us to protect future generations and build societies on a foundation of truth and accurate information. We all need them.

References

1. Brunner, C. and Tally, W. 1999. The New Media Literacy Handbook: An Educator's Guide to Bringing New Media into the Classroom. Doubleday: New York.
2. Crouch, D. 2017. The Importance of Media Literacy for Our Students http://edu.stemjobs.com/the-importance-of-media-literacy/Accessed 12 January 2019.
3. Hamilton, S. 2018. Developing 21st Century Skills: Information Literacyhttp://edu.stemjobs.com/developing-21st-century-skills-information-literacy/Accessed 12 January 2019.
4. Hobbs, R (2010). Digital and Media Literacy: A Plan of Action. (White Paper) Washington DC. The Aspen Institute
5. Koltay, T. 2011. The media and the literacies: media literacy, information literacy, digital literacy. Volume: 33 issue: 2, page(s): 211-221.
6. Kubey, R. W. 1997. Media Literacy in the Information Age: Current Perspectives. London: Transaction.
7. Menon S. 2018. How important is media literacy to students. https://www.edarabia.com/how-important-media-literacy-students/Accessed 14 February 2019.
8. Media and Information Literacy. UNESCO Institute for Information Technologies in Education. https://iite.unesco.org/mil/ Accessed 23 March 2019.

Chapter 8

Entrepreneurship

8. What is Entrepreneurship?

The Business dictionary defines entrepreneurship as the capacity and willingness to develop and manage a business with the intention to make profit. Westhead et al (2013: 6) say that entrepreneurship is "about what entrepreneurs do which involves:

- Assuming risk associated with uncertainty
- A person who supplies financial capital
- An opportunity creator and innovator
- A decision maker
- An industrial leader
- A manager
- An organiser and co-ordinator of economic resources
- The owner of an enterprise
- An employer of factors of production
- A contractor
- An arbitrageur
- An allocator of resources among alternative uses
- A channel for the spill over of knowledge from a knowledge organisation into a new firm to exploit the knowledge
- An alert discoverer or seeker of opportunities"

Entrepreneurial opportunities are everywhere and all individuals have the ability to be create and start a business and offer new products or services to society while making a profit. Creativity and innovation are important for entrepreneurs as they improve products and services in existence. You may read more about this in Chapter 3. Entrepreneurial firms are flexible and adaptable which enables them to seize new opportunities (Westhead et al 2013). (Also see chapter on Flexibility and adaptability).The problem of unemployment is a reality. It is becoming worse with thousands of graduates who are churned out every year in different tertiary institutions who cannot find employment. This is happening at the backdrop of shrinking economies. For this reason, young people across the world are being challenged to become entrepreneurs and not wait to find employment. Through entrepreneurship, you can contribute to economic development, reducing unemployment and poverty and generate wealth.

8.1 What Do Entrepreneurs Do?

According to Westhead (2013: 11) entrepreneurs engage in a number of activities namely:

- Stimulating competition
- Promoting lower prices
- Providing more consumer choice
- Encouraging creation and dissemination of new innovative products/services and/or better quality products and services

On the next page, is a diagram demonstrating what entrepreneurship is all about.

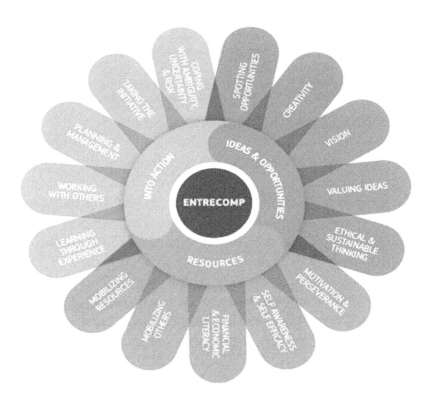

Source: https://www.eee-platform.eu/entrepreneurship-teaching-toolkit/

 It is true that not all businesses succeed. Some fail in the first year but eventually succeed. Other people try different ideas and fail in all of them. The difference between a successful and an unsuccessful business is implementation (how the idea is executed). Entrepreneurs accept risks, initiate new ways of thinking, are alert, explore new business and create new firms (Cuervo et al 2007).

To give yourself the best chances for success, you need to implement some strategies. Nieuwenhuizen (2004: 1) says that entrepreneurs know their strengths and weaknesses and if they lack the necessary expertise, they call on other people to help them. While this is good, you would eventually need to learn the language and vocabulary of the business and acquire as many skills as possible. Below is a section on some strategies that youths may employ to succeed in business.

8.2   Strategies for Succeeding in Business

1. Defining and evaluating one's goals

It is important to sit down and define what you want to embark on. For example if you want to go to Ezulwini from Mbabane, in Eswatini, you need to know what form of transport you will use (bus, car, or bicycle etc). If you decide to take the bus, you need to know where the bus rank is and go there. Thereafter you will get into the bus and drop off at the correct destination in Ezulwini. The same applies for one who wants to go from Manzini in Eswatini to Johannesburg in South Africa or to the Copper belt in Zambia. They need to be clear about the purpose of travel, what time they will go, how they will get there etc. In addition they need to have planned and be in possession of enough money for transport.

The same approach applies with starting a business, it is important to establish whether you want to get into production or servicing customers etc. It is important also to be clear about your motivation, know your capabilities and what you are willing to give up in order to start a business. Businesses involve taking risks, for example, financial risks. For this reason you should ask yourself if you are a risk taker and have a clear vision about your business and be prepared to lose money. Visionary people achieve good results than people who lack a vision.

2. Funding your Business

Before a business can gain a solid foundation, you need to secure some funds/resources to start the business and operate it until it stabilises. If you do not have the money to start, you would need to identify an entity, person or way to raise these funds. It could be a bank, some investors, crowdfunding or taking a loan. Some people have devised innovative ways of raising capital. Crowdfunding is one example, where would be entrepreneurs collect donations from family, friends, strangers, businesses and more. They use social media to raise awareness (ibid).

You should be cautious with personal information and funds raised online as you may be a target for criminals. It is important to find the best crowd funding platform that addresses your needs. Alternatively, you can also seek a business partner who already has money and sell them some company shares. The advantage of selling shares to someone who already has successful business is that they come into the business with vast experience which enables the business to grow and succeed faster. Capital and risks are shared between you and your business partner. In Africa, we still have opportunities to create crowding funding sites that emanate from Africa. Individuals in any part of the world can set up their cause for crowd funding. Below are examples of crowd funding sites.

8.3   Examples of Crowd funding Sites

Name	Website address
Gofundme	www.gofundme.com
Indiegogo	www.indiegogo.com
Kickstarter	www.kickstarter.com
Fundly	https://fundly.com
JustGiving	www.justgiving.com

3. Getting relevant experience and skills

There are a number of skills that you would require to run a successful business which you can acquire through shadowing a business owner in the same industry or getting an internship within the same field. Such skills including financial literacy, selling, marketing, good management of customers and employees among others.

4. Testing the idea for viability/Doing research

It is critical to test if the market is there for the business you intend to venture into which is sometimes called a feasibility study. You need to garner interest for your business/establish if your idea is feasible, without investing too much capital first. It all starts with the idea of a business. A business solves an existing and not imaginary problem. You may need to start by getting orders first and then supply potential customers. Never assume that a lot of people will buy your product or service because you like the idea or know one or two people who want the product or because your family likes it. In other words, researching the idea is very important to get the true picture of the situation.

5. Avoiding procrastination

Procrastination has no results. It is important to get on with the idea once you have researched it, registered and gotten the necessary clearances. Do not wait to put all the pieces together. Bear in mind that entrepreneurs take risks where others would not. You should avoid being perfect from the get go as perfection and growth will come with time.

6. Marketing the business

For a business to succeed, people have to know about it. For this reason, vigorous marketing is fundamental. But it all starts with knowing the fundamentals of marketing. Great marketers are fearless, approach people, are creative and provide value and know what to say to people. You may never know if your product or business will succeed until you start selling it. "Leaders use the conviction based selling method, which comes from their passion towards the area of expertise which creates a pull effect and demand towards his/her products or services" (www.entreprenuer.com).

You should leverage on the popularity of social media platforms to market your business. Uploading valuable content on these platforms will garner interest and sales from across the world. For example videos, podcasts and infographics are different kinds of materials that you can upload online about your products. Partnering with complementary businesses will enable your business to acquire credibility from others. Traditional forms of advertising such as on television, newspapers and radio is also important for boosting sales.

7. Communication

Communication is very important in the success of businesses. Powerful public speaking skills are important if you will promote your business. Some guidelines for communication include:

- Speaking purposively
- Helping clients solve problems by providing them with solutions
- Providing clients with wise practical advice
- Creating an elevator pitch i.e. give a speech that is short, simple and to the point
- Sharing your main point by telling them what you will teach them, teach them and remind them what you taught them
- Being convincing
- Learning from others
- Tailoring messages to suit specific audiences

Source: www.earlytorsie.com/10-ways-to-make-your-speeches-more-powerful-and-persuasive/

Robert Kiyosaki, American businessman and author, is the founder of Rich Dad Company and Rich Global LLC which offers financial and business education through books and videos. He argues that the old advice of getting a good job, saving money and getting out of debt is bad. (www.richdad.com). He says youths should get financial education and understand about investing and creating wealth (ibid). To succeed (I have selected points relating to business), he encourages getting relevant experience, designing the business properly (not design a business that will require you to keep pouring in money). Acquiring assets and not have too many liabilities. I have seen young people lose hope when the economy fails. They sit and fold their hands and wait for a miracle to take place. Instead when things are not going well economically, it is the time to be creative and to innovative. It is the time to see opportunities where others see problems and offer products and services that solve existing problems.

8.4 Qualities of Successful Business People

- Ability to deal with uncertainty
- Perseverance
- Self-motivated
- Take initiative
- Not afraid or pulled down by criticism
- Self-reliant
- Creative/innovative
- Offer value through their businesses

Entrepreneurs contribute immensely to the economy, job creation and fighting poverty. You can become a successful entrepreneur if you think positively, and be innovative. Take the challenge now.

References

1. Cuervo, A. Ribeiro, D. Roig, S. (eds) 2007. Entrepreneurship: Concepts, Theory and Perspective. Berlin: Springer.
2. Iversen, J. Jorgensen, R., Malchow-Møller, N. 2008. Defining and Measuring Entrepreneurship. Hanover: Now.
3. Roper, S. 2012.Entrepreneurship: A Global PerspectiveNew York: Routledge.
4. Royal Science and Technology Parkwww.rstp.org.szAccessed 15 January 2019.
5. Westhead, P. and Wright, M. 2013. Entrepreneurship: A Very Short Introduction New York. Oxford University Press
6. www.richdad.com Accessed 12 February 2019.

Chapter 9

Financial literacy

9. What is Financial Literacy?

Financial literacy is a skill important for all individuals. Financial literacy skills are about wealth creation, investment, management of one's finances, saving among others. Financial literacy enables you to be financially free (taking ownership of your finances and not be burdened with debt). Some people are born into poverty and die in it due to lack of a strong financial foundation. Others are taught that wealth creation and money are evil and therefore do not strive to be successful and to create wealth.

Most people grow up being told that acquiring a job and working to make a living is the only way to success. They get a degree, and get a job but continue to suffer throughout their lives because the salary is not enough which forces them to borrow. Very few people have financial freedom and are free from debt. Youths graduate with a heavy student loan while public service workers remain in debt throughout their life. Fewer people have multiple income streams because they are not afraid of taking risks and take initiative.

American billionaire businessman Kiyosaki says that most people focus on how much they make and pay less attention to how much they keep yet it should be vice versa (Kiyosaki 2019). There are stories of lottery winners who became millionaires and became poor again etc because they lacked knowledge and skills in managing their finances. Summarising Kiyosaki's 's *Rich Dad Poor Dad*, Schools (2019) identifies the following as the 5 essential takeaways for anyone looking to broaden their views on money.

1. Investing in Assets and not Liabilities

An asset is something that puts money into your pocket, while a liability is anything that costs money or takes money out of your pocket (an expensive car or television set). This distinction is important to make if you are to succeed. You should minimise expenses (liabilities) and invest in assets which will bring money into your pocket and not take out money by buying liabilities.

2. Experience Critical for Financial literacy

To be financially smart, Kiyosaki says mastering accounting, investing, markets and the law are very crucial. You should broaden your skills in order to be successful (Schools, 2019). "Knowing what to do with money when you get it, how to keep people from taking it from you is called financial aptitude" (Kiyosaki 2017: 90).

3. Learning to Sell

Selling is a crucial skill for generating wealth. You should practice selling and networking in order to be able to run your own business. Sales training courses are important to achieve this.

4. Fear and Self-doubt the Greatest Barriers to Success

Avoiding risks, self doubt and fear do not lead to success. You should be bold if you want to succeed in your endeavours.

5. Always thinking in Terms of Opportunities

Lack of a financial foundation, according to Kiyosaki is the reason why the poor and middle class are fiscally conservative. In the book, the "rich dad" forbids his kids from saying, "I can't afford it." Instead, he tells them to say, "*How* can I afford it?" The first phrase shuts down a person's brain, and they no longer have to think. The second one opens up "possibilities, excitement and dreams." It forces the brain to search for answers.

9.1 Tips for Financial Security

- Avoiding over spending on luxurious items and impulse buying
- Knowing how much you have and how much you can spend is important to ensure all essential needs/bills are paid for
- Building a strong savings plan ensures you have money when you need it most
- Developing a budget and sticking to it
- Creating automatic savings ie. Savings money should go directly into your savings account without first reaching your hands. There are banks which have these facilities, eg. First National Bank (FNB) etc.
- Not being afraid to negotiate for goods and services
- Keeping up with financial news so that you review your own commitments with time
- Taking good care of what you have acquired so that you do not have to buy the same thing multiple times eg. shoes, furniture, pots etc.
- Distinguishing between needs and wants so that you do not spend unnecessarily

9.2 How to Become Financially Literate

As we have already said, financial literacy is important for all individuals. For you to acquire these skills you should:

- Visiting your bank for financial advice
- Enrol online for financial literacy courses
- Follow financial blogs or programs on television which tackle financial literacy issues.
- Watch You Tube videos or listen to podcasts on financial literacy.

The diagram below shows financial freedom vs debt.

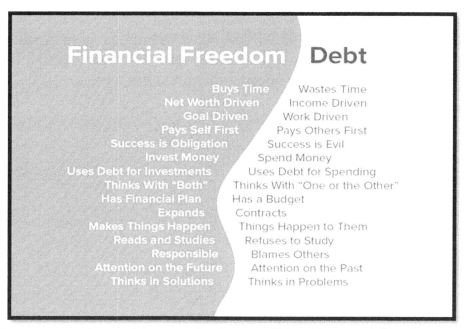

Financial Freedom / **Debt**

Financial Freedom	Debt
Buys Time	Wastes Time
Net Worth Driven	Income Driven
Goal Driven	Work Driven
Pays Self First	Pays Others First
Success is Obligation	Success is Evil
Invest Money	Spend Money
Uses Debt for Investments	Uses Debt for Spending
Thinks With "Both"	Thinks With "One or the Other"
Has Financial Plan	Has a Budget
Expands	Contracts
Makes Things Happen	Things Happen to Them
Reads and Studies	Refuses to Study
Responsible	Blames Others
Attention on the Future	Attention on the Past
Thinks in Solutions	Thinks in Problems

Source: https://www.oberlo.com/blog/financial-freedom

9.3   Examples of Saving Strategies

Starting to save as early in life as possible is important. Do not wait to start working or to run your own business to start saving. Some of the ways of doing this are:

- Forgoing luxurious spending eg, buying brand new cars, buying many cars, unnecessary trips, eating out, etc.
- Developing a budget and sticking to it.
- Investing in the capital markets
- Adjusting spending habits. When you do not have enough money to buy what you always buy, adjust. Do not force yourself to borrow money to buy petty things.
- Start a small project and work hard towards its success.

- Know that every little amount is important when it comes to saving. Do not say to yourself that I will start saving when I have a lot of money as that day may never come.
- Do not buy on impulse

It is important for all individuals to be equipped with financial literacy skills and achieve financial freedom. That way we will live debt free lives and save for uncertainties and after retirement.

References

1. 1. Ferreira, M. N. 2018. 10 Step Formula to achieve financial freedom in 2019 https://www.oberlo.com/blog/financial-freedom Accessed 29 October 2018.
2. Schools, D. 2019. This book about how to get rich sold more than 32 million copies- here are 5 essential lessons you need to know. www.cnb.com Accessed 20 March 2019.
6. These 12 Habits will help you reach financial freedom https://www.investopedia.com/articles/personal-finance/112015/these-10-habits-will-help-you-reach-financial-freedom.aspAccessed 12 February 2019.
7. Kiyosaki, R. 2017 and 2019. Rich Dad Poor Dad. US: Plata
8. Norbert Mungwini. Finance Lecturer. Email Interview: 23 April 2019.

SECTION THREE:
SKILLS FOR
LIVING IN THE WORLD

Chapter 10

Lifelong learning

10. What is Lifelong Learning?

The late former South African president and global icon, Nelson Mandela, once said that education is a powerful tool which can be used to change the world. It empowers, unlocks hidden potential and drives economies. You should continue to learn throughout your life. According to UNESCO, lifelong learning is based on integrating learning and life. It includes learning activities for people of all ages, in families, schools, community and the workplace. This means that irrespective of age, ethnicity or gender, you have no excuse of not learning in order to broaden your knowledge in a variety of fields.

Before the advent of the internet, people learnt in schools and colleges. They registered, paid fees, bought uniforms and attended classes. To date this is the practice. What is novel is how the internet has opened up a wide range of opportunities for learning. You no longer need to continue studying within the same career path as there are a wide range of subject areas which will help you make sense of issues holistically.

Example

If you graduated with a Geography degree, you can decide to take on courses in Legal studies in order to acquire knowledge in the discipline

Or

If you graduated with an Economics qualification and you want to do courses in Journalism and Mass Communication or Media Studies you can do so online and enrol for courses such as *Journalism, the future and you* and *Become a Journalist: Report the News* offered by Michigan State University (MSU), which are found on the e-learning platform Coursera. The courses cited above can broaden your knowledge in journalism.

There are young people who are holders of Law, Finance or Biology Degrees and are passionate about other subjects besides journalism and e-learning would provide them with the opportunity to fulfil their dreams. In the traditional set up you would have been expected to travel and enrol with the university. The internet eliminates time and space boundaries since you no longer need to be available at a particular geographical place at a certain time in order to learn or participate in an event. There are many online learning sites which offer courses which any young person can do for free or by paying a minimal fee for a certificate verified by the institution offering the course at the comfort of your home. For this reason, I want to challenge you to continue studying until the end of your life. Acquiring degrees is not sufficient in this technological era. Before providing links to the sites, it is important to outline some of the benefits of e-learning.

10.1   Benefits of Learning Online

Learning online has a number of benefits explained below:

- **Studying a Programme of Your Choice**

As alluded to earlier, the internet offers thousands of courses across subjects. Young people can choose courses of their choices online whether they have a previous qualification or not. Even if they have dropped out of college, they can still study a program they wish. In traditional schools, the flexibility to move from one discipline to another is non-existent.You can be told that you do not qualify or have the necessary background. With online education, this can no longer be the case as individuals enrol for a course of their choice.

- **Convenience**

Online learning does not require one to attend classes for long hours and interact with a teacher and other students in the same room and time. For instance, a student staying in Mbabane in Eswatini, does not need to travel to Manzini to do an online program. Similarly, a student in Zimbabwe does not need to go to Lesotho to do an online course. Instead all lectures and the needed materials are available via online platforms. This is unlike traditional classrooms where attending classes physically is necessary or when one has to travel from one place to another, find a place to stay in the place where the university is located and go to class. Online resources are easily available anywhere and at anytime and come in various forms such as word/pdf documents, audio visual materials, podcasts, slides and many more. Course instructors may also be available at specific times to answer questions. This can also be done anytime in social media groups created for specific courses.

- **Learning Multiple Courses Simultaneously**

Employers today are looking for people who are well versed in a wide range of subjects because of the complexity of problems being faced today. Through online learning, you can achieve this. A curriculum vitae (CV) with a list of online courses demonstrates that you are is i)broadminded ii) a life-long learner iii) committed to learning iv) eager to advance yourself educationally.

In the 21st Century, it is not enough to be 'one dimensional' or to be a one way street. Individuals need to show that they value learning. The University of Eswatini (UNESWA) and other universities and colleges in Eswatini do not offer Neuroscience, Acturial Science or Fine Arts. This should not hinder those interested in these programs from studying them. If you cannot afford enrolling at traditional universities in other countries to pursue subjects of your dreams, you can search online and enrol. Some traditional institutions do accept credit for courses earned via Massive Open Online Courses (MOOCs), i.e. freely accessible and open licensed short courses offered to learners online. The University of Edinburgh has up to two million people signed up for MOOCs (www.ed.ac.uk) and the courses are comparable to a standard University of Edinburgh course in terms of content and study level. The courses are led by world-class academics and supported by teaching assistants. A brochure for MOOcs offered at Edinburgh can be found at www.ed.ac.uk. Statements of participation are offered for those who enrol for free. Some of the courses offered, the number of learners and certificates awarded are shown in the table below.

Name of course	Number enrolled	Certificates awarded
AstroTech: The Science and Technology behind Astronomical Discovery	33 995	485
Philosophy and the sciences: Introduction to Philosophy of Cognitive Sciences	13 701	257
Animal Behaviour and Welfare	95 056	3237

Code yourself! An introduction to Programming (learners and certificates given).	124 139	910

Source- www.ed.ac.uk

For programmes that come with practicals, some institutions offering online courses have made arrangements with local institutions (closer to where learners are) to go and do practicals. It is also up to you the learner to seek internships and mentors so as to acquire the requisite skills. It is important to mention that not acquiring skills is no excuse for being inefficient at the workplace. You should always set yourself to be highly successful by doing your work with excellence.

- **Learning Online is Self-Paced/Self Directed**

When studying online you can direct your learning. Unless a course runs for a fixed time, you can take the course as and when you wish and do the reading and the assessments at a time that suits them. In traditional universities and colleges there are regulations about how much time you should enrol for a program, including attending lectures and tutorials and writing tests and other assessments. If you fail to meet some important requirements, you can be discontinued. In some situations, employed youths are unable to go back to colleges physically to take up new programs. They either lack the time to go back or the employer forbids them to do so citing staff shortages. Online learning enables individuals to overcome these challenges. Mothers and fathers can study online at a time convenient to their daily programmes.

- **Low Cost**

Studying online is much cheaper if compared to traditional colleges and universities. Some people have dropped out of college because they ran short of funds in the middle of the program. Some have completed programs but still carry the burden of a heavy debt which they continue with for most of their lives. Online courses are either free or charge very little tuition.

Example

The online learning platform Alison offers a Diploma in Public Relations in which one pays for different certificates between 400 and 700 South African rands. The Certificate and transcripts are emailed to you electronically or they can be sent via air (for you to get an original copy).

Being unemployed is no longer an excuse for lack of self-advancement because there are courses you can do online for free and use the qualifications to apply for jobs and compete with graduates who have studied full time and enjoy lives that are free of debt. It is up to you to check a variety of institutions that offer online courses that go in relation with their goals.

Interacting and Sharing Knowledge with others

Knowledge sharing with people from diverse backgrounds/ contexts is an important aspect of online learning. According to Heap (2017) you can interact with the course instructor and mates from a variety of countries or a diverse range of backgrounds. For example a Zimbabwean based learner, can interact with those in Malawi, Eswatini, South Africa, Paraguay, India, the United States of

America, France, Ireland, Singapore among others without the need to meet face to face. Online platforms have discussion forums or discussions can be done on social networking platforms such as Facebook and Twitter.

- **Self Discipline and Responsibility**

Heap (2017) notes that online learning teaches you to be self motivated and to manage time. In the 21st century, employers seek individuals who are self-motivated and also have good time management skills. Successful completion of online courses shows evidence of good time management together with self-discipline.

Improving one's Technical Skills

Computer skills are fundamental to completing an online course. When doing an online course you will be able to i) create and share documents ii) incorporate audio-visual materials. https://oedb.org/ilibriarian/10-advantages-to-taking-online-classes/

Computer skills are also important in the digital era as a lot of organisations use technology in their day to day activities. If you are seeking to advance yourself educationally you should do the following:

- Have basic knowledge of working with different kinds of documents; Microsoft OfficeWord, PDF, and audio visual materials (Also see Chapter 17 on Information Communication Technology (ICT) skills.
- Have knowledge of how Learning Management Systems (LMS) work. e.g. Moodle etc.
- Upload and download materials online
- Navigate the internet
- Have a functional email address

- Possess excellent typing skills

10.2 Disadvantages of Online Learning

- **Requires Reliable Internet Connectivity**

In Africa there are still areas which do not have electricity and internet infrastructure. Individuals residing in rural areas, who make up a huge percent in most African countries, are thus unable to take part in online learning unless they move to urban areas with reliable internet resources. This is a great disadvantage to learners who reside in the rural areas who come from poor families. While this may be the case, you should create opportunities for self-advancement in order to break the poverty cycle, hence the purpose of this book. It is not good for you or anyone else to blame their past, background or poor family for their lack of success. Opportunities come to those who find them. You need to stand up and create opportunities for yourself and future generations to come.

- **Courses Offered in English**

Most online courses are offered in the English Language which excludes those who have no understanding of this language. This challenges educational institutions to consider developing programs in local languages. In African universities, educators should consider offering online courses in languages such as Swahili, SiSwati, IsiZulu, IsiXhosa, ChiShona, Bemba, Shangani among others so that programs are relevant to local contexts. English is the official international language and you need to perfect your skills in it so as to be able to work in any part of the world.

Non-completion of courses

As alluded to earlier, studying online requires individuals who are self-motivated and who can manage their time well. Without these skills completion of courses will be far from achievable.

10.3   Websites Offering Online Courses

Name	Website address
Academic earth	http://academicearth.org/
Alison	https://alison.com/
Coursera	https://www.coursera.org/
edX	https://www.edx.org/
Khan Academy	https://www.khanacademy.org/
MIT OpenCourseWare	https://ocw.mit.edu/index.htm
Open culture	http://www.openculture.com/freeonlinecourses
Open Yale Courses	http://oyc.yale.edu/
Udacity	https://in.udacity.com/
Udemy	https://www.udemy.com/
Skillsshare	https://www.skillshare.com/
Saylor Academy	https://learn.saylor.org

Stanford Online	https://online.stanford.edu
Ted-Ed	https://.ed.ted.com/
UMass Boston Open Course Ware	ocw.umb.edu/

NB. This list is not exhaustive. There are many other sites and institutions offering opportunities for online learning. Individuals may search the internet for courses linked to their future plans.

10.4   How Online Classes Work

Different universities and colleges offering online courses do so on LMS. Examples include Moodle, Blackboard, Canvas among others. A number of universities in Africa use Moodle for blended learning purposes. They upload PowerPoint slides, course curricula etc on these platforms. As mentioned earlier online chats/discussion forums promote interactivity with the course instructor and among the learners.

Successful young people should consider online courses as opportunities to broaden one's knowledge in a variety of areas, opportunities to set themselves apart from the rest by showing ability to learn across disciplines. Young people should embark on life-long learning in order to broaden their knowledge in a wide range of subjects. Parents alike, and any interested individuals should do online programs so as to motivate the youth.

References

1. Broadbent, B. 2002. ABCs of e-learning: Reaping the benefits and avoiding the pitfalls. https://elearningindustry.com/5-advantages-of-online-learning-education-without- leaving-home
2. CollegeData (2016) What's the Price Tag for a College Education? College Data: Your Online College Advisor (online). Retrieved from https://goo.gl/fxQIF. Accessed 12 January 2019.
3. Heap, T. 2017. online.illinois.edu/articles/online-learning/item/2017/06/05/5-benefits-of studying-online-vs-face-to-face-classroom. 5 June 2017. Accessed 12 January 2019.
4. Lifelong-Learning.www.unesco.org/new/en/Santiago/education/lifelong-learning. Accessed 15 February 2019.
5. OEDb (2012) 10 Advantages to taking online classes. Open Education Database (online). Retrieved from https://goo.gl/aRZTRFAccessed 12 January 2019.

Chapter 11

Leadership

11. Leadership

Leadership skills are very important for young people seeking to advance themselves. No organisation wants to hire a follower or someone who will take the back seat. Leaders possess certain qualities that are important for taking organisations forward. Even when it comes to entrepreneurship, leaders know what actions to take or which doors to open in order to take the business forward. In other words, they possess leadership skills which are essential for success in the 21st Century.

Leadership skills come with experience and time. Leaders come from diverse backgrounds and have a large range of personalities; some are outgoing and friendly while others are calm. Many successful leaders have learned their leadership skills from the influence of mentors and they continue to improve on their skills and keep themselves motivated in order to remain of value to an organisation.

11.1   The Importance of Leadership Skills

Leadership skills are important for a number of reasons below:
- For building strong teams within a business and ensure projects, initiatives or other work functions are performed successfully.
- Good leaders motivate and inspire others while increasing employee engagement
- Supporting a positive environment and removing obstacles for their team.
- Encourage teamwork
- Making effective and ethical decisions

11.2   Improving your Leadership Skills

For you to be called an effective leader, you need to work hard and display the qualities identified above in your work. These skills do not come overnight. They take time and commitment. There are a number of strategies that you can employ if you wish to improve your leadership skills.

- Do self studies on leadership by reading on leadership, listening to podcasts and watching videos on good leadership which are readily available online.
- Participate in leadership training courses, workshops or clubs.
- Find a mentor. Mentorship is a good way to learn from those who have vast experience especially for young people.
- Study leadership styles you admire.
- Surround yourself with leaders. Businessman Jim Rohn, once said "You are the average of the people you spend the most time with."

11.3   Highlighting Leadership Skills in Applications

When you apply for opportunities, highlight where you have displayed your leadership skills as this is what employers look for. You can do this through:
- Incorporating key leadership traits you possess that are may be valuable to future employers, e.g. taking initiative and the ability to motivate and solve problems.
- Presenting leadership skills in sections such as work experience, key skills and achievements.
- Showing the leadership skills you possess in the cover letter. by picking one or two accomplishments and describe which skill you used and what the outcome was. For example, *if you were the project manager for an important initiative, you might*

explain how you brought the team together around a shared goal and show the success of the project.

11.4   Characteristics of Good and Bad leaders

Summarising ideas from Adair (2007), Kellerman (2004) and Burns (2012), good and bad leaders possess different characteristics.

GOOD	BAD
Visionary	Lack vision
Successful	Fail
Always willing to learn even from subordinates	They know it all
Communicate effectively across mediums and environments, good listeners and give feedback	Possess poor communication skills, do not listen and do not care about giving feedback
Take the blame and always give credit	Its all about them (possess pride and are arrogant
Show empathy, humility and kindness	Lack empathy and kindness
Focused and pay attention to detail	Lack focus and attention to detail
Bring change and innovation and lead their organisations to growth	They are static

Do not take the back seat or be a follower in life. Opportunities come first to those who take the front role. Taking initiative and being self driven are good leadership qualities. Below is a diagram on skills of leaders.

Source: https://www.thebalancecareers.com/top-leadership-skills-2063782

References

1. Adair, J. E. 2007. Develop Your Leadership Skills. Kogan Page.
2. Burns, J. M. 2012. Leadership. Open Road Media
3. Leadership skills: Definitions and examples. https://www.indeed.com/career-advice/resumes-cover-letters/leadership-skillsAccessed 10 January 2019.
4. Pitchford, P. 2014.21st Century Skills: A Vital Foundation for Students' Success https://www.leaderinme.org/blog/21st-century-skills/Accessed 12 January 2019.
5. Kellerman, B. 2004. Bad Leadership. What It is, How it happens and why it matters.
6. Key Skills of the 21st Century: an evidence based review https://education.nsw.gov.au/our-priorities/innovate-for-the-future/education-for-a-changing-world/research-findings/future-frontiers-analytical-report-key-skills-for-the-21st-century/Key-Skills-for-the-21st-Century-Analytical-Report.pdfAccessed 12 January 2019.

Chapter 12

Stress Management

12   What is Stress?

Stress is when the body responds to pressure from a situation or a life event. When you feel stressed, you become nervous, tense and on edge. There are a number of factors that lead to stress, social and economic challenges, family pressure, poverty, lack of money and many more. Many young people go through stress, after a break up, when they do not perform well at school, when a parent or guardian is sick and many other times. You may experience stress at home, school, college etc. All individuals (adults, youths and kids) do or have undergone some stress at some point in their lives.

When individuals undergo stress, they fail to concentrate, or progress, some fail to eat while others tend to eat too much. Some go to the extent of trying to commit suicide when they feel that the problem is too big to handle. Stress can also affect one's health, from experiencing headaches, back pain and cardiovascular issues (https://www.forbes.com/sites/forbescoachescouncil/2018/04/13/overcoming-stress-eight-things-professionals-should-know/#6c01f0f131f6).

You need to know that which is causing you stress in order to be able to develop mechanisms for coping with it. If it is homework, it is important to either approach the teacher or someone who can help you to do it. France (2014) says that goal setting is one of the ways of coping with stress. There are many other ways of coping with stress such as meditation, positive thinking, time management, talking with friends and taking breaks. Below is a list of some of the strategies you can use to manage stress.

12.1 Dealing with Stress

isit skinnyms.com

Source: https://www.pinterest.com/pin/153263193555460573/

Various scholars suggest different ways of dealing with stress, the ones mentioned above and others. Below I have elaborated on the strategies listed above and included others.

1. Meditation
Meditation is a practice where you focus your mind on a particular object, thought or activity in order to achieve a mentally clear and emotionally calm and stable state.

2. Avoiding caffeine, alcohol and nicotine

Caffeine and nicotine are stimulants which can increase the stress level rather than reduce it. When alcohol is taken in smaller quantities, it also works as a stimulant which can increase stress. You are advised to take in water, teas or natural fruit juices as they help the body to cope better with stress. Healthy, well balanced and nutritious diets are encouraged at all times.

3. Engaging in physical activity

Physical exercise can help restore the body of a calmer and more relaxed state. When you are undergoing stress, it is always advised that you take a walk and get some fresh air. Increased levels of oxygen trigger the release of feel good hormones that help relieve pain and induce feelings of pleasure. Taking deep breaths is thus important for dealing with pressure. Physical activity improves one's quality of sleep.

4. Getting more sleep

A lack of sleep can cause stress. It is important to maximise on relaxation before going to sleep. The bedroom should be free from the things that cause stress. Sleeping at the same time is important for the body to get used to a particular routine everyday. Reading a book or taking a warm bath can help in the calming process while caffeine and excessive alcohol can lead to disturbed sleep.

5. Trying relaxation techniques

Words such as "calm" "love" and "peace" work well, or you could think of a self-affirming mantra such as "I deserve calm in my life" or "Grant me serenity". Focus on your chosen word or phrase; if you find your mind has wandered or you become aware of intrusive thoughts entering your mind, simply disregard them and return your focus to the chosen word or phrase. If you find yourself becoming tense again later, simply silently repeat your word or phrase.

6. Talking to someone

Talking to someone about how you feel can help alleviate stress. Talking works by distracting you from stressful thoughts or releasing some of the built-up tension by discussing it. In schools and colleges there are counselors and psychologists who help students to overcome stress.

7. Keeping a Stress Diary

Keeping a stress diary for a few weeks is an effective stress management tool which will help you become aware of the situations which cause you to become stressed. In the diary a young person can note the date, time and place of each stressful episode, with whom you were with and how you felt both physically and emotionally. The diary can later be used to understand what triggers your stress so as to avoid stressful situations and develop better coping mechanisms.

8. Managing your time

Prioritising work and tasks to be done is very important. If there are tasks that can be delegated you can do so. Always get into the habit of recording tasks according to when they need to be done. One also has to create buffer times to deal with unexpected and emergency tasks and also include time for your relaxation and well being.

9. Learning to say "no"

Learning to say "No" to additional or unimportant requests is important to reduce stress levels and may help you to develop self-confidence. Some people are unable to say "No" because they want to help and are trying to be nice and liked. For others, it is due to fear of conflict. There are phrases that individuals can use to let down other people more gently. For example:

"I am sorry but I can't commit to this as I have other priorities at the moment"
"Now is not a good time as I am in the middle of something. Why don't you ask me again at...?"

"I would have loved to help you but...."

10. Resting if you are not well

If you are feeling well, it is important to get some rest so that the body may recover.

11. Taking control

It is important to develop skills of solving problems and come up with solutions. Writing down a problem and coming up with as many solutions as possible and finally selecting the best solution and implementing it can also help lower stress. Laughing or adding humor helps relieve stress.

Source: https://www.skillsyouneed.com/ps/stress-tips.html

12.2   Stress at School and Work

At school, stress can be caused by too much work (assignments, reading materials etc with very short deadlines. If you fail a course or grade and have to repeat it again next year, you may find yourself stressed. Or if your friend, decides you can no longer be friends that can be difficult to handle and may lead to stress. Stress in the workplace is common and is caused by many different factors, including excessive hours, conflicts with others, feelings of isolation or when an under qualified person is offered a job you thought was for you. You will continue to be stressed until you admit that it was not meant for you.

12.3   Getting help for stress

Your doctor or psychologist or counselor can help you deal with stress (schools and colleges have their own counselors)

12.4   Benefits of Overcoming Stress
- Helps eliminate unnecessary energy drain.
- Maintains stored resiliency.

- Impatience, irritability, anger decrease.
- Improves physical and mental health.
- Greater access to intuition.
- Memory, focus, other brain functions improve.
- More energy in daytime, restful sleep at night.

Source: https://www.heartmath.org/resources/solutions-for-stress/reducing-stress/

References

1. France, R.C. 2014. Introduction to Sports Medicine and Athletic Training (3rd edition)
2. Nordqvist, C. 2017.Why stress happens and how to manage it. https://www.medicalnewstoday.com/articles/145855.phpTue 28 November 2017.
3. Stress https://www.mentalhealth.org.uk/a-to-z/s/stressAccessed 12 January 2019.
4. 5 Things You Should Know About Stresshttps://www.nimh.nih.gov/health/publications/stress/index.shtmlAccessed 12 January 2019.
5. What is stress? http://www.stress.org.uk/what-is-stress/Accessed 10 January 2019
6. Stress https://www.betterhealth.vic.gov.au/health/healthyliving/stress Accessed 9 January 2019.
7. Stress https://kidshealth.org/en/teens/stress.htmlAccessed 9 January 2019.
8. Dealing with Stress- Ten Tips. www.skillsyouneed.com/ps/stress-tips.htmlAccessed 10 January 2019.
9. https://www.forbes.com/sites/forbescoachescouncil/2018/04/13/overcoming-stress-eight-things-professionals-should-know/#6c01f0f131f6 Accessed 10 January 2019.

SECTION FOUR:

PERSONAL SKILLS

Chapter 13

Flexibility and Adaptability

13.   What is Flexibility and Adaptability

Flexibility according to the Cambridge English Dictionary is the ability to change or be changed easily according to a situation. Adaptability refers to the ability to deal with change. The highly changing environment of the 21st Century requires graduates who can adapt to changing circumstances and environments. Flexibility is among the top skills that employers seek today. You should show that you are flexible and deal with change and uncertainty.

13.1   What Flexibility involves

- Adapting successfully to changing situations and environments
- Keeping calm in the face of difficulties
- Planning ahead, but having alternative options in case things go wrong
- Thinking quickly to respond to sudden changes in circumstances
- Persisting in the face of unexpected difficulties
- Anticipating and responding positively to changing environments
- Ability to adapt to change positively in response to changing circumstances
- Taking on new challenges at short notice.
- Dealing with changing priorities/workloads

Source: www.kent.ac.uk

13.2   Showing Adaptability on your CV

You can show adaptability on your CV through a variety of ways. Below I have listed some of the ways:

- Stating that you have lived in another country
- Working a part time job while studying
- Changing holiday plans at the last minute

You should always be in position to show your employer or business partners that you are flexibility and adaptable. This can be done by doing the following:

- showing willingness to learn new methods, procedures, or techniques and take on new tasks
- Showing initiative & self-reliance
- Looking for new ways of doing things and to achieve objectives.
- Making suggestions for increasing the effectiveness of changes.
- Being resourceful with a positive, 'can do' attitude to change.
- Responding with energy to new challenges, the unfamiliar and the unexpected.
- Looking for ways to make changes work rather than identifying why change won't work.
- Adjusting your methods to deal with a changing situation or emergency.
- Shifting your priorities in response to the demands of a situation.
- Not being frightened to improvise. You are comfortable about moving into action without a plan: planning on-the-go.
- Being tolerant of time pressure, working well close to deadlines.
- Bounce back from setbacks and maintain a positive attitude.
- Keep an open mind.
- See the bigger picture.
- Like variety.

- Be good at multi-tasking (doing a number of tasks at once): juggling a number of balls at the same time.

Source: https://www.kent.ac.uk/ces/sk/adaptability.html

References

1. University of Kent. Flexibility and Adaptability https://www.kent.ac.uk/ces/sk/adaptability.htmlAccessed 10 January 2019
2. University of Leeds. Communication and Interpersonal http://careerweb.leeds.ac.uk/info/4/make_yourself_employ able/202/employability_skills/5Accessed 10 January 2019

Chapter 14

Being Positive at all times

14.   Avoid Thinking Negatively

A problem which pulls down most young people in the 21st Century is thinking negatively and not believing in one's self. Negative thoughts are destructive and do not bring about development. They bring fear and they can make you narrow-minded. You should avoid the negative thoughts listed below. When you have negative thoughts, strive to turn them into positive ones.

14.1   Negative vs Positive Thoughts

Negative thoughts	Positive thoughts
"I never do anything right"	I will do this right
"I will never make this work"	I will make it work
"This will never work"	It will work nomatter what
"I was never meant to succeed"	I will succeed
"I am not good at anything"	I will be good at this one
"I am bad at everything"	I will be good at this one

Successful people do not think negatively. Instead they are positive minded about life and they always make things work in their favour. A positive attitude makes an optimist, takes away worry and negativity. According to Brian Tracy, rather than saying you have a problem, you should say

"I have an interesting challenge facing me"

And you should go about saying positive words to yourself such as:

" I like myself"
"I love my work"
"I feel happy"

14.2   What is a Positive Attitude?

- A mental state that expects the best to happen
- Positive thinking
- Always believing that things will turn out well
- Actively finding solutions to problems
- Optimism
- Motivation- the energy to accomplish goals
- Brings about perseverance
- Happiness and contentment
- Looking at failure and problems as learning curves
- Not being discouraged by negative thoughts, comments and people
- Believing that there is light at the end of the tunnel
- Seeing setbacks and stress as temporary

Source: www.successconsciousness.com/positive-attitude.htm

References

1. Sason, D. and Sason, R. Positive Thinking- The Power to Succeed. Learn How Becoming a Positive Thinker Would Improve Your Life.
2. www.successconsciousness.com/positive-attitude.htmAccessed 12 April 2019.
3. Tracy, B. www.entrepreneur.com / article/282965. 4 Ways to maintain a positive attitude Even when you are stressed.

Chapter 15

Physical Fitness, Wellness & Positive Lifestyle

15.   What is Physical Fitness?

Physical fitness is the body's ability to function efficiently and effectively in work and leisure activities without fatigue. After doing work, a person should quickly recover and be able to perform some more work. Optimum efficiency is the key to physical fitness. As a young person seeking success in life, it is important that you remain physically fit.

Physical fitness is one of the core pre-conditions of active health. You cannot be healthy without being physically fit. If you are suffering from any perceptible disease, then you are considered physically fit. Physical fitness of young people is different from that of the aged. The physical fitness of a sports person is different from that of the persons working in an army or a layman. In fact, physical fitness means different things to different people.

15.1   Importance of Physical Fitness

The quality of your life will improve when you consciously adopt a healthy lifestyle which promotes physical fitness as follows:

- improves the functioning of heart and lungs by increasing the availability of oxygen to all tissues and organs in the body system;
- improves muscle tone;
- promotes the development of good posture, proportionate figure, and thereby positive body image and physical appearance;
- ensures quick recovery after injury and illness;

- decreases the risk of chronic and cardio-vascular diseases; (diabetes, heart attack, Asthma, etc.)
- reduces and controls undesirable body fat. When you exercise, take a proper diet that also fulfils nutritional requirements, you will maintain an ideal body weight;
- reduces depression and anxiety;
- postpones fatigue and reduces recovery time after vigorous activity;
- helps people to meet challenges of life

Being physically fit is important for all age groups. To live life to the fullest and enjoy all the opportunities, physically fitness is crucial. To achieve fitness, various modes and methods can be used. Before adopting such methods, warming up before activities and cooling down after activities are essential to minimise any risk of injuries.

15.2   What is Wellness?

Wellness is an active process of becoming aware of and making choices towards a healthy and fulfilling life. It is more than being free from illness. The World Health Organisation (WHO) defines wellness as a state of complete physical, mental, and social well-being, and not merely the absence of disease or infirmity. As a young person, it is important to ensure that your entire being is well.

15.3   What is a Positive Lifestyle?

Lifestyle is a way of life or style of living that reflects the attitude and values of a person or group. A positive lifestyle means a positive attitude and taking positive action which focuses on solutions, not on problems. When you fail, you have to keep trying again and again and not lose enthusiasm. You have to live in the present, making the most of it, and not dwelling on the past or worrying about the future. Most youths like to cry over what their parents could not provide for them or their background. They blame other people for their failures and never see good in others. It is important to remain positive and focused. Noticing the good traits of others and not just their negative ones is important. This requires that you stop criticising and judging people and being more kind and helpful.A positive lifestyle therefore means a positive outlook and viewpoint, expecting the best, and striving to do the best you can.

You do not need money, possessions or fame to live this kind of life. A positive lifestyle does not depend on your circumstances, where you live, and what you do for a living. It depends on a positive attitude and state of mind. You can adopt this kind of lifestyle, irrespective of your financial situation, age, work or circumstances. You can live a positive lifestyle, even if you have problems and difficulties and your life conditions are negative.

15.4   Benefits of Physical Fitness, Wellness and a Positive style

- Physical fit people do the work required of them with ease
- Motivate and encourage others
- Keep going especially when there is pressure and uncertainty
- Live a longer life
- Have a purpose in life and are able to achieve dreams

References

1. Bouchard, C., Blair, S. N., & Haskell, W. L. 2006. *Physical activity and health*. Champaign, IL: Human Kinetic.Google Scholar
2. Bouchard, C., & Shephard, R. J. 1994. Physical activity, fitness and health: The model and key concepts. In C. Bouchard, R. J. Shephard, & T. Stephens (Eds.), *Physical activity, fitness and health, International Proceedings and concensus statement* (pp. 77–88). Champaign: Human Kinetics. Google Scholar
3. Campbell N.,De Jesus S., Prapavessis H. (2013)Physical Fitness. In: Gellman M.D., Turner J.R (eds) Encyclopedia of Behavioral Medicine. Springer, New York, NY. DOI: 10.1007/978-1-4419-1005-9_1167
4. Caspersen, C. J., Powell, K. E., & Christenson, G. M. (1985). Physical activity, exercise, and physical fitness: Definitions and distinctions for health-related research. *Public Health Reports, 100*(2), 126–131.PubMedGoogle Scholar
5. Larson, L. A. (1974). *Fitness, health, and work capacity: International Standards for assessment*. New York: Macmillan.Google Scholar
6. Warburton, D. E. R., Nicol, C. W., &Bredin, S. S. D. (2006). Health benefits of physical activity: The evidence. *Canadian Medical Association Journal,* 174(6), 801–809.PubMedCrossRefGoogle Scholar
7. UCDavies. Student Health and Counseling.https://shcs.ucdavis.edu/wellness/what-is-wellness

Chapter 16

Tolerance and Mutual Respect

16.   What is Tolerance?

The Cambridge English Dictionary defines tolerance as the willingness to accept behaviour and beliefs that are different from your own, although you might not agree with or approve of them. Other definitions say it is the ability to deal with something unpleasant or annoying or to continue existing despite bad or difficult conditions.

16.1   Types and Examples of Tolerance

Example	Type
Tolerating different political viewpoints	Political tolerance
Tolerating different religious viewpoints	Religious tolerance
Tolerating children's behaviour	Tolerance towards children

Tolerance is needed in all life spheres, socially, politically, economically, at home, school, church and everywhere where there are people. We live in a 'global village' where people of different backgrounds, religions and cultures co-exist. Societies are becoming more multicultural as people migrate from one continent to another in search of opportunities for business and work. Youths are also migrating to seek work, internships, mentorship and educational opportunities. South Africa is an example of a multicultural society with people of various nationalities staying together. Nigerians,

Zimbabweans, Somalis, Ethiopians etc may all be found in South Africa. There are other countries which are also multicultural. We see and live with diverse individuals in our workplaces, school and business. For this reason, exercising tolerance is an important skill of the 21st Century.

UNESCO declared the International Day for Tolerance in 1995 with the objective of generating public awareness of the dangers of intolerance and to help people understand the importance of tolerance. You should realise that all humans have rights and no human being has power to violate the rights of another. As you seek opportunities in different parts of the world, be open minded and continue to learn about other cultures including various languages. As indicated in the Chapter 10 on Life Long Learning, it is important to enrol for courses online for self advancement. Courses on learning other languages are there online including those on tolerance. The onus is on you to seek such opportunities.

16.2   Examples of Lack of Tolerance

Everyday we see stories in the media of people attacking others because of differences in their skin colour, viewpoints, ethnicity, religious beliefs etc. You will remember the hatred and killing of foreigners in South Africa in xenophobic attacks in 2015, 2018 etc. During elections, different parties clash over divergent viewpoints. This is not good at all. Below is a diagram depicting global oneness.

Source: http://zazenlife.com/2017/11/10/tolerance/

16.3 Promoting Tolerance

To be more tolerant there are things you can do such as:

1. Finding more knowledge and being educated about other people's customs and culture
2. Being more respectful of others
3. Avoiding stereotyping other people
4. Being open-minded
5. Teaching children and young people at an early age that every person is distinctive in some way.

16.4 Qualities of Tolerant Individuals

Tolerant individuals exhibit important skills as they interact with people from diverse backgrounds. Some of the qualities have been listed below:

- Humility
- Showing respect
- Being open minded

- Always seeking knowledge and understanding about other cultures.
- Travelling and learning about other cultures will help you to become more tolerant.

16.5   Importance of Tolerance

As we have already indicated, the importance of tolerance cannot be overemphasised. Tolerance is important for reasons as listed below:
- Promoting love and peace among diverse people while preventing fighting and violence.
- Remaining focused. Hatred and intolerance of humans that are different from you leads to loss of focus on one's goals.
- To be successful in life. When you focus on your goals and are focused on achieving them, you will succeed in your life.

References

1. Atif, A. L. 2010. Importance of Tolerance. www.timesofmalta.com
2. 2. Bird, C. (1996) Mutual Respect and Neutral Justification, Ethics, 107:1, pp. 62–96.
3. Callan, E. (1997) Creating Citizens (Oxford, Oxford University Press).
4. Connolly, W. E. (1995) The Ethos of Pluralisation (Minneapolis, University of Minnesota Press).
5. 5. Defining Tolerance. UNESCO https://unesdoc.unesco.org/ark:/48223/pf0000232631 Accessed 10 January 2019.
6. Tolerance: the threshold of peace. A teaching / learning guide for education for peace, human rights and democracy. 1994. http://www.unesco.org/education/pdf/34_57.pdf Accessed 12 January 2019.

Chapter 17

Conflict Resolution and Negotiation

17. What is Conflict?

Conflict is a serious disagreement between two people as a result of various issues. It could arise from disagreements, misunderstandings or miscommunication.

17.1 What is Conflict Resolution?

According to Shonk (2019) conflict resolution is the formal/informal process of finding a solution to a dispute.

17.2 What is Negotiation?

It is a process of settling differences while avoiding arguments and dispute. From the above definitions, we can argue that conflict resolution and negotiation are the same as they are both about finding solutions to disputes.

When working, staying or studying with other people, conflict is inevitable. You may find yourself angered by something or you may need to mediate a dispute between two people in your department or college. In business, you may be in conflict with a client or customer. Conflict is normal because as individuals we cannot always agree on issues.

When managed well, conflict can strengthen the bond between those who were initially in disagreement. Managing conflict can help prevent harm and help those involved to chart a clearer way of how to progress in the future. If not managed well, conflict can result in permanent harm, the disintegration of families and relationships, the breakdown of businesses and loss of focus.

17.3   Conflict Resolution Skills

1. **Managing Stress (Also see Chapter 12 on Stress Management)**

When you remain calm, you avoid uttering words with are hurtful which can permanently damage the relationship. It may prevent you from harming yourself.

2. **Managing your own emotions (Also see Chapter 4 on Emotional Intelligence)**

Managing your emotions is an important skill of dealing with conflict. If for example you realise that you are too angry and want to fight a collegue, it is advisable to move away, calm down and go back to the colleague at a later time or the following day. By the time you go back to the colleague you would have had enough time to think about the situation and consider the options you have to deal with the situation and the potential outcomes.

3. **Negotiation**

Negotiation skills are of paramount importance. You are expected, in different situations to be good negotiators. Effective negotiation requires that enough research is carried out in order to know all the pertinent facts of a situation in order to arrive at a best possible outcome.

4. Improving non-verbal communication (see Chapter 6 on Communication)

A calm tone of voice, a reassuring touch or concerned facial expression can help to defuse heated exchange. It is always important to be aware of your non-verbal communication and to also make sense of that of the next person so as to avoid conflict.

17.4   Avoiding Conflict

There are a number of ways of avoiding conflict. Below is a list:

1. Being a good listener. Always understand first what has been said before overreacting.
2. Seek clarity and give the next person the right of reply at all times.
3. Being aware of your emotions and controlling them.
4. Encouraging the next person to share his/her point of view as fully as possible and if they decide to be quiet, respect that until they talk when they are comfortable.
5. Do not assume/run into conclusions
   Some examples of statements you can say in conflict situations are
   "I wasn't to understand what has upset you"
   "Can you say more about that"
   "Is that how it usually happens"

Source: University of Wisconsin, Madison

References

1. John W. Burton 1990. Conflict: Resolution and Prevention Author: New York: St. Martins Press.
2. R. A. Akindele and B. E. Ate (eds) 2002. Beyond Conflict Resolution. Lagos: Nigerian Institute of International Affairs.
3. Fisher, R. J. 1977. Interactive Conflict Resolution. New York: Syracuse University Press.

Chapter 18

Social Manners

18.   What are Social Manners?

When growing up, we have been taught to behave in certain ways so as to show respect to others. These rules of behaviour are called social manners. For example saying thank you, please, excuse me, I am sorry among others.

18.1   Personal Appearance

The way you look plays a significant role in your success. Whether you are at school, going for an interview or at the workplace, it is important to present yourself in a manner that is professional and appropriate to your industry/school. Dressing well will increase your self confidence and impress those that you stay and work with. There are some important rules you should follow such as the following:

- **Following the school or company dress code**

It is important to establish what the school, company or university dress code is as soon as you join that institution. If there is none, observe how others dress and also be guided by the kind of work you do. Office work requires you to dress formally. This is important especially these days where casual wear is becoming popular. Part of dressing smart for work includes wearing fresh, clean and properly ironed clothes.

- **Ensuring that your clothes fit**

Too small or too big/loose clothes will not make you look good. For example if you are wearing tight shoes, co-workers will be quick to notice that you are wearing small shoes by the way you walk (limping or showing discomfort). Tight skirts, tops and trousers will also not look good.

- **Avoiding being too sexy**

Inappropriate clothing may be too distracting to colleagues and may give an inaccurate impression. You should avoid too short hemlines, plunging necklines and exposing under garments. Remember that through your dress, you are communicating values about yourself.

- **Keep your hair tidy, clean and appropriate**

Your hairstyle should be appropriate to your workplace. If working at food outlets, laboratories, and medical fields. It is advisable to tie your hair to avoid hair falling everywhere. Do not leave the house with wet or uncombed hair and ensure that your jacket/top is free from hair and dandruff after combing. Ensure that your braids are clean and tied well. Beard should be kept short and neat in order to maintain a professional look. Do not be lazy to shave as too large beard can make you look scruffy. Usage of shampoo can help your hair to become healthy and clean.

- **Wearing pantyhose**

Pantyhose has become popular for those who wear formal. It can make you have a more finished look.

- **Wearing shoes that are polished and in good condition**

Ensure that your shoes are in good condition and polished at all times.

- **Avoiding ankle socks with trousers**

When you cross your legs and pants slightly lift up, no skin should show. Ensure that your socks are of an appropriate length. The same applies to wearing pantyhose, full socks are usually better that knee highs.

- **Do not over- accessorise**

You should avoid over accessorising. For example having rings on every finger, too many bangles etc and ensure that your jewellery does not make noise.

- **Wear rich colours to portray authority**

Darker colours (black and navy blue) are better than lighter ones. Also avoid too bright clothes.

- **Keeping teeth and nails clean**

Your teeth and nails should be kept clean at all times. Visit the dentist regularly and avoid bad breath problems by using mouth wash.

Source: https://www.businessinsider.com/rules of appearance

18.2 Interacting with others

When with colleagues or classmates, you should interact well with them. When you meet people for the first time, you should begin by introducing yourself and stating why you are there. You can also extend a firm and confident handshake. Be aware of your body language. Positive body language includes maintaining eye contact with the person you are talking to. Avoid talking too much. Instead, talk, listen and give feedback.

Do not scroll your cellphone while talking to others. Checking messages will make you appear less interested in the conversation with the person in front you. If you phone rings, it is courtesy to ask the person you are with to take the call. When in an office and a person, knocks and comes in, stop whatever you are doing and give them attention. If you are on the phone, you may give them a signal to sit down, and ask them to finish off the telephone conversation and talk to them. Avoid talking to visitors with your back facing them as it makes you appear less interested in them. Also in an office setting, keep your phone volume low and turn off notifications on social media. Always be gentle to others by being more caring and avoiding anger.

18.3 Dating

Dating etiquette varies from culture to culture and is influenced by a number of factors. If you are dating a person whom you are already familiar with, you will find yourself being free to talking about any topic and the experience will be different if the person is new. For example if you have met him/her online. While there are no strict rules about the appropriate age to start dating, you should be clear why you should be dating. Do not be pressured into dating someone if you are not interested and be frank about how you feel.

18 is taken as the legal adult age but nowadays many youths will still be going to school and trying to find their feet at this age. Delaying dating while you are at school is therefore advised. It has become common for individuals to date at work or while at internships. If you are at internship it is advisable to avoid dating colleagues or supervisors as things can get very complicated, affecting your professional relationship and how you relate with other colleagues. Remember that you are at the organisation for purposes of learning. When you start dating colleagues, you may lose focus on your main goal. In the event that you start dating, there are some basics things you may want to bear in mind:

- Remain true to yourself
- Meet the person in an open area where there are other people. E.g. in a restaurant
- Be clear to the next person about what you are looking for
- Do not be judgemental
- Make eye contact
- Do not use your phone unless you are expecting an important call or message and notify the other person about that
- Ask questions and listen attentively
- Do not be afraid to leave if things get awkward
- Be prepared to pay the bill/share the cost if you have to

18.4   Meal Time Manners

Different cultures observe different rules of what is expected of individuals during meal times. Obisakin (2007) says rules of behaviour are important in order to avoid conflict between different cultures. There are however some basic rules of behavior if dining with others. Below is a table on the dos and don'ts during meal times.

Dos	Don'ts
Sit properly (and straight) in your chair	Don't talk about gross things
Talk about pleasant things	Don't ask for seconds before others have had firsts
Place your napkin on your lap	Don't take more than your fair share
Wait until everyone is seated before starting to eat	Don't overload your fork or plate
Watch others, or ask, if you're not sure how to eat something	Don't gobble your food
Ask someone to pass the food, rather than reach across the table	Don't chew with your mouth open
Chew with your mouth closed	Don't talk with your mouth full
Don't talk with your mouth full	Don't play at the table
Say "excuse me" or "I'm sorry" if you burp	Don't hum or sing at the table
Say "no thank you" if you don't want a certain dish or are full	Don't tip your chair or lean on the table
Say "may I please be excused" before leaving the table	Don't eat with or lick your fingers

Source: http://mtstcil.org/skills/manners-1.html

18.5   Some Important Occasions

While you are at work or school or during your internship time, it is important to be at your best behavior. Show love and care to others. Be respectful to colleagues. Do not be bossy or nosy into other people's issues. At end of year parties, avoid taking in too much alcohol or eating too much to the point that people have to carry you home. Do not take drugs. Avoid parties which end very late. If a party goes on until late, be in the company of others. Always ensure to maintain some form of professional distance when you attend an event in which your supervisors will be attending.

References

1. Rules of Appearance in the Modern Workplace. https://www.businessinsider.com/rules-of-appearance-in-the-modern-workplace-2013-11 Accessed 12 April 2019.
2. How Important is Appearance in the Workplace. https://www.skillsportal.co.za/content/how-important-appearance-workplace Accessed 12 April 2019.
3. Personal Appearance. https://www.skillsyouneed.com/ips/personal-appearance.html Accessed 12 April 2019.
4. 5 Science-Backed Personal Appearance Tips to Look Your Best https://letsreachsuccess.com/science-personal-appearance/ Accessed 14 March 2019.
5. Obisakin, L.O. 2007. Protocol for Life: Guidelines on Diplomatic, Official and Social Manners. Ibadan: Spectrum Books.

Chapter 19

Collaboration

19.   Defining Collaboration

The Cambridge English Dictionary defines collaboration as the process of two or more people working together to complete a task. If you are aiming success, you should strive to work with others. Collaboration involves sharing tasks, ideas and the work to be done and the end product is owned by all members of that group. Levin (2018) says collaboration is what drives successful businesses. Openness and clarity are important for groups to effectively work together. It requires all the people involved to put their effort and brains in one project.

There are some individuals who do not know or fully understand the process and benefits of collaboration. When they are given a group task, instead of putting all their brains and effort in producing one product, they break down the tasks and each one goes their way, there is no sharing of ideas and at the end, individuals own the specific task they worked on. It is important to work collectively and share ideas if you are to work on a project or assignment with others. There is more power in working together and the product is much better than can be done by individuals. At school, teachers give assignments which they expect to be done by all members of the group. Similarly, you will find yourself assigned to work on a project with others at work and you should be able to know what to do. Below are steps of the collaboration process.

19.1   The Collaboration Process

1. Build trust
Fostering trust between members will bring about good collaboration. Members also need to be comfortable with credentials of each other from the outset
2. Getting together

Setting goals, timetables and individual responsibilities are important to avoid misunderstanding and not delivering on deadline.

3. Using collaborative tools
Throughout a project, teams can use collaborative tools to communicate. These tools allow for sharing feedback in an open and constructive way. For example, groups can create online groups designed for keeping communication lines open. Facebook or WhatsApp groups are examples of such groups and members do not wait to be at the same place in order to communicate. They continue to share ideas, pose questions, share videos, images and podcasts relating to that project.

Get together again
Towards a project's conclusion, it is important to get together to discuss the progress and share experiences.

4. Track and share results
The results of the project should be owned by all members of the team.

19.2   Collaboration advantages

Collaboration comes with many advantages such as promoting teamwork, members of a group inspire and motivate one another, it encourages more creative input and results in a successful project. If you have an opportunity to work with others, do so, so that you improve your chances of success.

Below is a diagram that depicts collaboration benefits.

Source: https://www.skmurphy.com/blog/2009/06/28/michael-schrage-on-innovation-collaboration-tools-and-incentives/

19.3   Disadvantages of Collaboration

- **Competing to lead**

When you have a collaborative group, you may sometimes end up with too many people trying to take the lead which can cause tension among the rest of the staff, including those that may not even be involved in the collaborative effort. It is thus important to give each other opportunities to perform tasks and support one another as opposed to competing to do a specific task.

- **Conflict**

Conflicts may also arise due to differing working styles and approaches to work.

19.4   Skills needed in Effective Collaboration

Teamwork

Compromise

Tolerance

Communication

Flexibility

Reliability

References

1. Hansen, M. T. 2009.Collaboration: How Leaders Avoid the Traps, Create Unity, and Reap Big Results. Boston: Harvard Business Press.
2. Hewett, B. L. and Robidoux, C. 2010. Virtual Collaborative Writing in the Workplace: Computer-MediatedCommunication Technologies and Processes. Hershey: IGI Global.
3. Huxham, C and Vangen,S. Managing to Collaborate: The Theory and Practice of Collaborative Advantage. London: Routledge.
4. John-Steiner, V. 2000. Creative Collaboration. Oxford: Oxford University Press.
5. Johnsen, H. C. G. and Ennals, R. 2012. Creating Collaborative Advantage: Innovation and Knowledge Creation in Regional Economies. Surrey: Gower
6. Schuman, S. (ed.) 2006. Creating a Culture of Collaboration: The International Association of Facilitators Handbook. San Francisco: Jossey Bass.

SECTION SIX: INFORMATION COMMUNICATION AND TECHNOLOGY (ICT) SKILLS

Chapter 20

Using various ICT tools

20.   Microsoft Office Skills

In today's technology world, it is important for you to show your prospective employer that you are competent with various ICT tools including Microsoft Office. This is the most basic requirement for all individuals seeking to develop themselves. Microsoft Office skills require you to show competence of Microsoft Word, PowerPoint, Excel and Access.

Microsoft Word	Microsoft PowerPoint	Microsoft Access	Microsoft Excel
Source: https://alison.com/course/microsoft-word-2010-revised-2017	https://www.pcworld.com/article/3018735/check-out-powerpoint-2016s-best-new-features-charts-effects-and-more.html	https://www.logolynx.com/topic/access	https://teaching.cambriancollege.ca/studio/microsoft-excel/
Creating official documents such as letters, memos, reports etc	Doing dynamic professional presentations at work or school	Storing and analysing data	Spreadsheet for doing calculations by adding formulas
Including tables and graphs and other diagrams	Designing banners	Creating databases that are easy to use. (Including name, phone, age, work details)	Doing substractions and additions etc
Adding photos etc	Combining audio-visual materials	Used in various workplaces, schools, colleges and hospitals or any organisations dealing with large data	Creating budgets etc
Creating books, newspaper articles and letters	Creating notes for students		Analysing quantitative research

20.1   Using the Internet for Self Advancement

There is no doubt that the internet and social media have become an integral part of our daily lives. Platforms such as Facebook, Twitter, Instagram and WhatsApp among others help us reach out and connect with millions of people worldwide. They can be used for self advancement or for career development with many positive results. There are many ways that social media can help you to grow your career if you use it correctly. Networking, job, internship, scholarship opportunities are some of the advantages of using social media as individuals across the globe post such information on a regular basis. It does not matter what your goals are and the field/discipline you are working in, social media offers a wide range of opportunities that are posted by individuals and organisations on a regular basis.

Always go online with the intention to find something that will take your career to the next level. When you go through individuals statuses and profiles do not become envious of their achievements. Instead, if they post pictures about a conference they attended, take time and note down the name of the conference, ask them how they got to participate and how you can be part of it in the future. You may even look for more information regarding the conference via Google so you get more information on what it is about, when next it will be held and how you can get involved.

Social media also provides opportunities for networking with people in various fields. We live in an era in which collaborating across disciplines is being encouraged. Do not take your Facebook friends for granted as they may be your avenue to your next destination. You may ask them what they do and seek opportunities to collaborate in research, community service etc. depending on your interests. Going online for purposes of entertainment only is not advisable if you seek to make a meaningful contribution to this world. The world today is seeking people that are driven and are willing to go the extra mile in order to solve problems. People who lack a vision end up as a liability in the workplace. There are some people who spend hours and hours on social media while at the workplace and this has detrimental results because they fail to meet deadlines and produce work that is below the expected standard.

Potential employers check profiles and statuses of potential employees online. You should clean up your status and ensure that it is free of offensive and hate speech. Also clean up images and videos that have graphic content and sex which you are tagged in. Always ask yourself the question, does my profile put my career in the best possible light? If your answer is no, take the time to tidy it up. Ensure that your posts are responsible and not in bad taste. You may consider posting motivational quotes and content that will not offend the next person such as jokes, news articles etc. It is fine to post what you do during your spare time and hobbies but ensure that this is done professionally. Find and connect with and follow leaders and organisations in your field and areas you are interested to venture into in the future.

Spending 15 minutes a day or week searching can net you hundreds of quality contacts. Make use of keywords on Facebook, Linked In or Twitter for a guarantee of the best results. You may also join groups that are committed to specific causes. Interacting with people in different social media platforms can be a source of great insights into establishing a new responsibility in your workplace, as well as help you improve your career. Get in touch with career professionals on Twitter or Facebook who will help you steer your career in the right direction. Like and comment on posts and images of companies, organisations and individuals you admire so that you get similar content in the future. If you are an entrepreneur, you can use social media to make business connections in order to grow your business. If you a running a blog about a topic of your choice, keep the content simple, avoid jargon and technical language. Make use of images, headings, and info-graphics to draw people in.

20. 2 Sending Professional Emails

Emailing has become the most common method of communication with potential employers, within organisations, sending applications etc. It is fast, cheap and it provides opportunities to attach important documents that make up the application package etc. When you write emails, always be professional. This means you start with a greeting such as *"Dear Primrose"*. Indicate your subject. Email platforms such as Yahoo and Google Mail will ask if you want to send the email without a subject line if you have not indicated one. State your purpose in a brief and concise manner. Use capitals when starting sentences and end with full stops. Ensure that your spellings and grammar are correct. Do not use emoticons; only reserve them for personal emails. It is also advisable to keep the email as brief as possible and ensure that your font size is not too small or too big. You may use Calibri or Times New Roman for your font choice as they decent and not playful. In the event that you have a lot of information to share, you may use bullets for easy reading. Always end your email with a proper closing such as saying *"Thank you"*, or *"Yours Sincerely,"* or *"Kind regards"*.

20.3   How You should Use Social Media

You should use social media to seek opportunities for personal advancement, educationally and for business etc. The internet is sometimes called a library of libraries because of the wealth of information it offers. In terms of education, you can go online, open a website of a university of your choice anywhere in the world and apply for admission. For example, if you want to study at the University of Illinois, in the United States of America, the website will provide information on courses on offer, duration, funding support and scholarships, staff, future employment opportunities etc. The same applies if you want to study at Bergen University in Norway, University of Zimbabwe (UZ), in Zimbabwe, Simon Fraser University in Canada, Makerere University in Uganda, University of Cape Town, (UCT) in South Africa, Kenyatta University in Kenya, University of Zambia (UNZA) in Zambia, Singapore University in Singapore among others.

- **Establishing a business and engaging with customers**

In terms of business development, you can have access to information on organisations that fund start ups, join groups for youths in business, link up with successful young business people in the world etc. Such opportunities will only be available to you if you seek them online. Taking initiative thus becomes of paramount importance. You may set up an online business and engage with customers online. There are individuals who are making money by providing coaching services online. This can be done on Instagram, YouTube, Twitter, Facebook or many more.

- **Joining Discussion Forums**

There are a lot of social movements that stand for a number of issues that affect society positively. You should join these groups, and start non-governmental organisations among others. You might have observed young people who spend hours and hours on social networks just chatting on unimportant issues. If you were among them, it is important for you to do some introspection and minimise on the time spent discussing triviality. The internet and social media offers plenty of opportunities for career advancement, including business.

- **Motivational purposes**

You should follow successful motivational groups/pages on Facebook, Twitter or Instagram. It is important to stay motivated in order to remain positive and focused. One motivator once said that motivation was like bathing, it has to be done all the time. The quote is true, always inspire and challenge yourself by reading motivational books, quotes, listening to podcasts and watching videos. All these can be found online.

20.4   Addiction to WhatsApp and Facebook can destroy your life

Spending hours and hours on Facebook, WhatsApp, Instagram and Twitter browsing through photos, statuses and chatting with friends is a destructive habit we want to discuss. This habit can lead to anxiety disorders and can make you feel inadequate especially through exposure to information of the 'good' things that are happening in friends' lives. For example, going to vacations, being taken out to dinner by their spouse, hanging out with friends and having fun etc are some of the most common posts we come across on social media. Often times, we then compare with our own situations and feel inadequate. A university of Houston study found out that buying into people's postings on social media can lead to symptoms of depression. It is therefore wise to minimise the term you spend online so that you do not buy into people's postings regarding what is happening in their lives.

The other problem which comes with spending many hours online is accessing and sharing pornographic and other indecent materials that are sent into our inboxes or which we see on friends' profiles. It is important to not create such materials let alone share them.

When you see content online, do not believe it because you have come across it. It is wise to first establish its veracity before you can take any form of action. There are individuals online whose main role is to create and share false information. Be aware of that and take cautionary measures whenever you are online. If you are not sure of something, ask experts. In Chapter 7, on Media and Information Literacy there is information on how to distinguish between fake and credible information.

20.5   Avoiding Social Media Addiction

In order to be productive and fulfil your life dreams, you will need to limit the number of hours you spend online. This will help you avoid addiction. Below are strategies you can employ to avoid being addicted to social media:

- Reducing the amount of time spent on social media for social networking/
entertainment purposes

- Disabling sound notifications in order to avoid disturbances
- Occupying yourself with important assignments such as studying/reading, being productive at the workplace
- Avoiding usage of the phone in class, during important family times such as during meals and when in the presence of other people.
- Not taking your phone with you into the bedroom. Remember the bedroom is for sleeping and not for chatting. Also avoid waking up in the middle of the night to check new messages and notifications. Discipline is critical if you are going to minimise the time you spend online.

20.6   Social Media for Success

It is important that you use the internet and social media to establish your pathway to success. There are positive stories on the internet and in books of people who have leveraged on these platforms to build successful businesses, to link with potential employers and get the jobs they have always wanted among others. Following motivational speakers has provided others with a source of inspiration so that they keep going and remain focused on their goals. Whenever you log onto your social media platforms always challenge yourself to focus on that which will build your life, career and enable you to nurture successful and meaningful relationships.

References

1. Arulmani, G. Bakshi, J. A., Leong, F.T.L., and Watts, A. G. 2014. Handbook of Career Development: International Perspectives. New York: Springer.

2. Smith, D. Growing your Library Career with Social Media. London: Elsevier Science.

3. Waldman, J. 2013. Job Searching with Social Media For Dummies. New Jersey: John Wiley.

4. http://www.latimes.com/health/la-le-social-wellbeing-20150606-story.htmlAccessed 12 January 2019.

5. Why social media can be damaging for young people. https://news.sky.com/story/why-social-media-can-be-damaging-for-young-people-11513282 30 September 2018. Sky News. Accessed 10 January 2019.

SECTION SEVEN: CVS, RESUMES, PERSONAL STATEMENTS AND COVER LETTERS

Chapter 21

Writing a Winning Curriculum Vitae (CV)

21.   What is a CV?

A Curriculum Vitae (CV) is a detailed summary of professional and educational histories used for job, scholarship, fellowship applications etc. It lists one's demographic data, education, work experience and key skills. Potential employers use it to find out if one has the right experience, educational qualifications and skills for a job on offer. Employers go through hundreds of CVs for a job so it is important to get it right at all times. It is not a resume (see next Chapter on Resumes).

21.1   Purpose of a CV

- To market one's self directly to a prospective employer.
- To list your experience, qualifications and skills for a prospective employer to match against their job description.
- To entice an employer to want to learn more about you further and therefore offer you an opportunity for an interview.

NB. There is no one way or format of writing a CV. What is critical is to ensure that your CV details important information about who you are, your qualifications and achievements and is packaged in a readable format.

21.2   What should be in a CV?

- **Personal details**
This includes your full name in bold at the top, home address, a working email address (make sure it sounds professional) and not one such as sexygirl@hill.com . Prospective employers will

not take you seriously if you include such an email. Working phone numbers either a landline or mobile are important to include.

- **Education, professional qualifications and other training**

Including details about qualifications and your educational background is important, particularly if it is relevant to the job you are applying for. You should list your qualifications in order by most recent first. It is important to be as accurate as possible about what qualifications you have.

- **Current status and employment history**

This includes stating what positions you have held in the past and the skills you acquired in the process. You should list all your working experiences, both paid and unpaid, and the time you spent there, starting from the most recent. For every role, ensure that the job title and the name of your employer are as clear as possible. Write a brief description of your role and responsibilities for each position including your accomplishments. It may be easier to write this in bullet points. You should aim to have 3-4 points as part of each role.

- **Any skills and interests**

Detail the skills that are relevant to the job you are applying for showing how and when you used them. Computer (including internet and social media), communication and research skills cut cross professions. It is therefore important that they are included in your CV. For one applying for a Journalism job, it would be important to write skills such as research, news writing (both for hard news and feature stories), interviewing among others.

- **References**

A reference is a short testimonial from someone that knows you. This person is called a referee. It gives an employer a better idea of your reliability and ability to do the job. It is common for people to write *'references available on request'*. Identify people you are happy for a prospective employer to contact to get a better sense of you as a person, a student or as a worker. These are usually from the organisations you have previously worked for or where you have studied. However, you may want to include your referee's name and contact details on your CV. If you want to use someone as a reference, make sure you get their permission first so that they will be prepared to talk about you in case they are contacted. Do not leave out their contact details including emails as these will be used by the organization to ask for a reference.

21.3 Guidelines for writing a Winning CV, which will land you an interview

- Tailor-make your CV to suit the requirements of the job you are applying for. A one version suits all approach will not take you anywhere. In other words, you cannot use the same CV for all jobs, scholarship offers etc as they are unique and emphasise varying skill sets.
- Use font that is clear and readable, stick to the standard font size 12, Times New Roman, 1.5 spacing.
- Ensure that your CV has a clear layout so that it is easy to read for prospective employers.
- Use headings and subheadings to break up sections, and Bold and Italics to make your CV more readable or easy to follow.
- Bullet points are a good way to communicate everything quickly and clearly. Make use of them to keep sentences short and concise.

- Put your Name, Address and Contact Details clearly at the top of the front page to allow potential employers to find your contact details quickly.
- Write a Personal summary or profile which briefly outlines your key objectives, previous experience and important skills that are in line with the job you are applying for. It may start as follows: *"A highly motivated individual seeking ...."*
- List your Professional Experience and Education in reverse chronological order i.e. your most recent job / course studied at the top to allow whoever is reviewing your CV to gain a quick snap shot of what you have been doing most recently. Dates should also be included accurately.
- Include 2 or 3 referees addresses, position and company, email and phone numbers. Remember to contact them first asking for their permission and also to provide them with details of the job you are applying for
- Part time employment and community service or voluntary work are important to include
- Include a section on hobbies that you take part in regularly and any extra-curricular activities you took part in at school, like sports or music groups and provide specific details for these.

21.4   Characteristics of a bad CV

- Abundance of spelling and grammatical errors
- Written into one long document with no sections or subheadings to guide the reader
- Not making use of *Bold* to separate subheadings from general content
- Uses slang and informal language
- Does not include contact details especially email address and phone number (yours and your referees)

21.5   What to avoid in a CV?

Avoid including the following information:

- Your gender and age unless you have been specifically asked to include this information
- Putting your relatives as referees or people that are not linked to the jobs you have stated/ or where you studied.
- Not including your contact details especially the phone number and e-mail address
- "Informal" fonts like *Comic Sans. Think Arial, Helvetica* or *Gill Sans.*
- Lies, as you will be caught when later asked to talk more about it etc.
- Rambling with the purpose to fill up space. If you have nothing important to add, do not say anything.

21.6   Final tips

- Regularly update your CV with new employment experiences and qualifications so that you do not leave any important information out.
- Always tailor-make your CV so it suits the specific job you are applying for. Gear your CV towards the skills and experience required in the job advertisement.
- Be positive about yourself and sell yourself as much as possible
- Be in mind that you are competing with hundreds other applicants for an opportunity to be called in for an interview therefore give it your best shot
- Ensure that your CV is easy to read and keep it brief
- Do not leave key sections that relate to the job you are applying for as it makes it difficult for potential employers to assess you

- Ask someone else to check your CV for you so that they identify any errors or omissions
- Always keep a ready electronic and hardcopy CV for any quick requests

References

How to write a winning CV

http://downloads.bbc.co.uk/tv/makeit/Make_It_CV_Guide

Chapter 22

Writing a Winning Resume

22. What is a Resume?

It is a brief summary of personal, educational, professional experiences used for job applications. A well-written resume highlighting your most relevant qualifications for the job will help you get selected for an interview. Your resume needs to be consistent, concise, clear and easy to read. Resumes are usually 2 pages because they are not meant to include every detail of your past experience. Remember to only include relevant information due to space constraints. Your resume is meant to quickly highlight the reasons you're a great fit for the job.

Your resume should be tailored and updated based on the specifics of each opportunity to which you apply. Ensure that it draws more attention to your most applicable skills and accomplishments.

22.1   What Information should be in the Resume?

Contact information (Name, phone, email address, location, Linked In profile
Work experience
Education
Career summary
Skills
Volunteer work

22.2   How long should the Resume be?

Aim for a one page resume whenever possible and a maximum of 2 at the most. Remember that a resume is not a CV so it only highlights the most important information that is relevant for the position being applied for.

References

1. Michigan State University (MSU). Career Services Network. https://careernetwork.msu.edu/resources-tools/resumes/sample-resumes.html Accessed 12 March 2019.
2. Resume Writing Guide.https://www.jobscan.co/resume-writing-guideAccessed 12 March 2019

Chapter 23

Writing a Winning Personal Statement

23. Personal Statements

Personal statements are sometimes also called "application essays" or "statements of purpose". These are essays that are written in response to a question on a graduate application i.e. with the purpose of selling one's self usually for Masters or PhD. They vary in lengths from university to university. It is however important to note that they are written when one is applying to a highly competitive program such as Fulbright or any other scholarships offered by universities across the world. There are some highly competitive internship programs which also require applicants to submit personal statements or statements of purpose.

Because of the highly competitive nature of application processes, it is important to write a personal statement that will create and leave a lasting impression on the recruiters. The personal statement also has to be relevant to what you are applying for. It is the admissions team, which include Professors from the field you will be applying for that often sit in the admissions committees and go through all the applications identifying the best/top candidates. Like they always say, experience is the best medicine. The more one writes, the better they become in writing *winning* personal statements. In other words, one should apply more and write many more personal statements. I have emphasised winning in order to demonstrate that the personal statement should not be rated as ordinary, but it should be the one that wins the scholarship or internship opportunity that is on offer.

23.1 Writing a Winning Personal Statement

A winning personal statement is one that will take you to the interview level and give you an opportunity to tell the panellists why you are the suitable candidate for the position on offer. In it you should write what is stated below:

- Indicate what makes you unique or different
- Demonstrate why you are choosing that career path
- State your long term goals
- Show when you initially became interested in the career. How has this interest developed? When did you become certain that this is what you wanted to do including what solidified your decision?
- What are your intellectual influences? What writers, books, professors, concepts in college have shaped you? Some personal statements may stipulate that you should indicate what your research is about. This is where the intellectual influences will come in.
- What are two or three of the academic accomplishments which have most prepared you?
- What research have you conducted say at Master's or undergraduate level and how does it link with the one you want to do for the program you are applying for?
- What are your future career plans? How does graduate or professional school pertain to them?
- What's the most important thing the admissions committee should know about you?

23.2 Steps to take when writing a Personal Statement

1. Give yourself enough time to respond to the questions
2. Analyse the question(s) asked on a specific application.
3. Research the school and/or program to which you are applying.

4. Take a personal inventory. Write out a 2-3 sentence response to each question.
5. Write your essay.
6. Revise your essay for form and content.
7. Ask someone else - preferably a faculty member in your area - to read your essay and make suggestions for further revision.
8. Revise again.
9. Proofread carefully.

Source:http://www.cws.illinois.edu/workshop/writers/tips/personalstatement/

23.3   What you should Do?

- Start with the perfect opening statement (It may be a story or something that happened which links with the program of study)
- Ensure your essay is interesting and coherent
- Build an argument
- Show enthusiasm
- Ensure that your goals are well articulated
- Ensure that you demonstrate knowledge of your chosen field articulately
- Ensure that you state what you hope to benefit from the host institution if awarded the scholarship or opportunity
- Keep it concise, pertinent and to the point.
- Take your time
- Find a proof reader

23.4   What to Avoid?

- Spelling, grammatical and punctuation errors
- Slang
- Repetition

- Rushing it
- Emphasising the negative. Remember that you are trying to create an impression so be positive about yourself
- Footnotes, they are not necessary
- Statements such as "I've always wanted to be a..........." because they do not add value.

References

1. How to: Write a personal statement
   https://www.reed.co.uk/career-advice/how-to-write-a-personal-statement/ Accessed 15 April 2019.
2. How to write a UCAS undergraduate personal statement.
   https://www.ucas.com/undergraduate/applying-university/how-write-ucas-undergraduate-personal-statementAccessed 15 April 2019.
3. Writing tips: Personal statements
   http://www.cws.illinois.edu/workshop/writers/tips/personalstatement/ Accessed 15 April 2019.
4. 10 Tips for Writing a Personal Statement for University Applications https://www.topuniversities.com/blog/10-tips-writing-personal-statement-university-applicationsAccessed 15 April 2019.

Chapter 24

Writing a Winning Cover letter

24.   What is a Cover Letter?

It is your chance to expand on your CV and persuade the recruiter that you are the perfect person for a job and is usually 1 page long.

24.1   Steps of writing a Winner Cover Letter
- Research the organisation's mission and values, target market and history
- Start of by stating why you want to join the specific organisation
- Explain why you are the ideal candidate
- Demonstrate your motivation and enthusiasm in helping the organisation achieve its goals
- End with a positive statement

24.2   Crafting a Winner Cover Letter
- A great cover letter is tailored to a specific position or university being applied for.
- Make it stand out and impress the recruiter by showing your expertise and interest
- Show why the organisation/university is the best
- Highlight and expand on two to four qualities and experiences relevant for the role, do not reproduce what is in the CV.
- Show what you can deliver
- Provide concrete examples and solid numbers wherever you can.
- Make it concise with short and well structured sentences
- Ensure that it uses standard font and is free from grammatical, punctuation and spelling errors

- Tell a story that is not in your CV or resume
- Address the letter to one specific person in the company (It could be the hiring manager or Head of Human Resources and you may find him/her via Linked In

24.3   Final tips

- Make it short and concise.
- Demonstrate why you are the best for the position on offer and give specific examples
- Show why the organisation is the best
- Make the cover letter stand out
- Give yourself enough time to write one
- Give a friend to go through it and give you feedback

References

1. How to write a winning cover letter https://jobs.newscientist.com/article/how-to-write-a-winning-cover-letter/ 13 September 2018. Accessed 15 February 2019.

2. The 8 Best Cover letters You need to Read Now https://www.themuse.com/advice/the-8-cover-letters-you-need-to-read-now Accessed 15 February 2019

3. The Cover Letters That Make Hiring Managers Smile (Then Call You) https://www.forbes.com/sites/dailymuse/2014/02/06/the-cover-letters-that-make-hiring-managers-smile-then-call-you/#165c5d4745f1 Accessed 15 February 2019

Chapter 25

Online Applications

25. What are Online Applications?

It is now commonplace to do online applications in the technological era we are living in. Whether you are seeking a new job, scholarship, internship, grant etc you will most likely be asked by the institution concerned to complete an online application. You will be required to input all your personal details, including full name and surname, age, sex etc and to also upload your CV and academic and professional certificates including an image of yourself. There are important basics you should follow to successfully complete online applications. Online applications may be very time consuming but they require persistence for you to do an excellent job as you will be competing with thousands of other applicants.

- **Have a functional and professional email address**

You should have a working email address that you check regularly and it should have your name and if possible your surname. There are a number of email platforms to set up emails. Yahoo, Google (Gmail) and Hotmail are some examples. If you are Brian Green, your email address could be something such as bgreen@gmail.com or briang@yahoo.com etc. Avoid addresses such as sexyboy@yahoo.com or flirtyboy@hotmail.com

These platforms will sometimes suggest emails with numbers such as bgreen5@gmail.com and this does not matter. Such an email address will hinder you from your next opportunity to advance in your career. This is because scammers/hackers use such email addresses and using such an email will portray you as someone who is not serious.

- **Including a subject line**

If the site requires you to add a subject line, do so. Do not leave this section blank. You may include something like *"Application for Salesperson job"*.

- **Write a message**

In the space for a message you should write an appropriate, short and professional message. The first thing is to introduce yourself. Beckitt (2014) says that "this is where you need to make the employer want to find out more about you". In other terms, your message should make the recruiter want to read your resume or CV. Do not just say "Please find my resume attached". You can include information on the number of years of experience you have, state your achievements and qualifications briefly. You should bear in mind that the purpose is to entice the one who will read the CV.

Example
"Good morning I wish to apply for the position of XYZ as advertised on abc.com. With 6 years experience working at Fair Cosmetics as the Northern Region Sales Manager, achieving a 10% sales increase in the 2018 financial year. I am keen to discuss your available role and expand on my sales and management experience at interview. Regards, Sharleen.

Source: Beckitt, C. 2014. The basics of Online Job Applications: for the Over-50s and anyone on the job market. Booktango

Attach Important and Relevant Documents
Do not forget to attach important and relevant documents. It is best to attach Pdf documents because they will open the same way on the recruiter's computer as opposed to Microsoft Word (MsWord).This is because your recruiter may have a different version installed hence

information is bound to move positions thereby distorting the entire document making you appear disorganised. No recruiter would want to go through a distorted CV thereafter.

25.1   Guidelines for Doing Winner Online Applications

As more and more institutions are relying on online applications for recruitment, it has become significant for individuals to learn and develop the skills of successfully doing onlineapplications. In order to do winner online applications, that will land you interviews, there are a number of things that you will need to follow which are listed below.

- Always research and have as much information as possible about the organisation you are applying to before you start completing the application.
- Understand fully the requirements of the position you are applying for so that your answers are tailor-made towards what is important. Your answers (qualifications and experience) should speak directly to what the job is asking
- Respond to online applications as soon as possible to avoid rushing the process.
- Follow instructions given. For example if you are told to apply via email do so, if through the organisation's website do as instructed. Failure to follow instructions shows that even when hired, you will not follow instructions.
- Type out answers on a Microsoft Word (MsWord) document before and then paste them onto the spaces provided. That way you have time to work on it to perfection.
- Always attach important supporting documents such as a cover letter, work samples and certificates as required by the position.
- Ensure spellings, gramma and punctuation are done perfectly as small mistakes will make your application look weak.

25.2   What to Avoid

There are a number of things that you should avoid when doing online applications, which may hinder you from your next opportunity. It is the little things that can cost an individual from going a step higher on your career journey.

- Do not type a letter with grammar and spelling areas, ask a friend to proofread before you send.
- Avoid copying and pasting information from your CV without tailoring it to the requirements of the position you are applying for
- Do not submit an incomplete application as it will portray you in a negative light as someone who would not be able to complete tasks if hired.
- Do not complete an application without understanding what the position you are applying for requires.
- Avoid partially completing your application and then coming back later as it may affect the flow of your answers. It is always best to go through the questions first and allocate enough time so that you complete the application.

25.3   Your Online Profile, Video Applications in Emails and Social Media

These days, people have online profiles. It could either be on Linked In or you may create one on job portals. Facebook and Twitter also offer individuals opportunities to create profiles. Basics things which are important about your online profile are listed below.

- Ensure that your profile is up to date and summarises key information about your accomplishments.
- Make use of key words throughout the profile to increase chances of your profile appearing on searches. Eg. If you are in Computer Science, your key words would include terms such as *"coding"*, *"programming"* or *"coding"*, which are related

to your field. If in Library and Information Science, your keywords would be *"cataloguing"*, *"information management"* etc.

- Include a professional photo and ensure that its positioned well to fit the space provided
- Include information about where you are and what you are seeking
- Include recommendations as they strengthen your profile.
- Include links to videos showing you getting an award, doing community service or giving a presentation. In other words show the link to your e-portfolio.
- Include accurate contact details, including phone number and email address.

Due to the high level of competition, you may also want to be creative with your online application. You may contact potential employers and send them an email of yourself talking about who you are, your skills, qualifications and the kind of opportunity you are seeking. You may use your social media accounts to do the same particularly Linked In where potential employers will see you.

References

1.   Beckitt, C. 2014. The basics of Online Job Applications: for the Over-50s and anyone on the job market. Booktango
2.   How to Apply for Jobs Online https://www.thebalancecareers.com/how-to-apply-for-jobs-online-2061598. Accessed 20 January 2019.

Chapter 26

Succeeding at Interviews

26   What is an Interview?

An interview is your opportunity to demonstrate how you would be a good fit for a position on offer. It comes after you have gone through the first stage of applying. It gives you the opportunity to discuss your skills and experience in greater detail and, importantly, what you feel you could bring to the organisation.

26.1   Succeeding at Interviews

26.1.1 Before the interview
- **It all starts with preparation**

Do some background research on the company or the university you have applied to (Check the company website and social media platforms such as Linked In, Facebook and Twitter).
Review the job description and be clear about what you applied for
Understand the purpose of the organisation and the specific position you applied for
Think of examples that can demonstrate the skills they are looking for
Know what kind of interview it is- practical or oral/ telephone or Skype so you prepare appropriately.

- **Plan your travel**
It would be bad to getlost or miss the bus before an interview or arrive early and fail to find parking. Make sure you know where the interview is being held and how you are going to get there. This means checking the internet for directions or calling the organisation

to get specific directions on where they are located before the interview day.

> If the place is far and requires travelling the day before, do so in order to avoid delays
>
> Make a note of the person who will be interviewing you so that you can let them know if you are going to be late (*only if the unforeseen happens*).
>
> Leave early as it will help you to feel more prepared, and composed on arrival

- **Dress for success (plan what to wear)**

> Unless otherwise stated, prepare formal wear
> Black/blue suit, white shirt and tie for men
> Black/Blue and white blouse for women,
> Shined closed shoes are the best and not sandals
> Limit accessories
> Ensure that the clothes are well ironed and free of creases
> Make sure that it is your correct size; avoid too small or oversize clothing
> Avoid flowery clothing or printed clothing with messages on them or a logo of another organisation.
> Avoid revealing clothes
> The more professionally dressed you are, the higher your chances of feeling good and confident.

- **Ensure all your qualifications are in order**

> Some institutions want to see original certificates at the interview session
> Check and ensure that your certificates and transcripts are all there and are in good shape

26.1.2 At the interview
- **Do not panic; Be yourself**

Be polite and gracious to everyone you meet from the time you enter the organization premises to when you leave. You may never know who will be interviewing you.

While it is normal to be nervous, quickly gain your composure by taking a deep breath.

Avoid panicking as it will cost you the only opportunity you have to sell yourself

If a question throws you off track, ask for a moment to think about it and compose yourself.

Be yourself as that will make you more comfortable about your answers. It will also make you feel relaxed and appear genuine

Watch your body language (e.g.*Do not start biting your nails because you are nervous or play with your hair*).

Sit up straight and always look at your interviewer in the eye. If it is a panel of 4 people, look straight into the eyes of the one asking you a question at a particular moment

- **Answering questions**

Listen carefully and provide an answer which is the most appropriate

Do not answer a question with an answer that does not relate it (Memorised answers might not be well suited for a particular question. Just because that is what you had planned to say, does not mean you have to say it where it does not relate

Do not be afraid to ask the interviewer to repeat the question if you did not hear clearly

Provide different examples for different questions in order to show your communication or teamwork skills

When given the opportunity to ask questions, do so. e.g. How many people are in the team I may be working in?What is the best thing about working there? When can I expect to hear your decision?

Look interested and leave on a positive note

> Do not appear bored
> Smile and nod and thank the panel for the opportunity for an interview
> Remain enthusiastic
> Be professional

26.2 Examples of Interview Questions and Guidelines for Answering

1. Tell us about yourself

Do not be tempted to give a short response instead use this time to introduce yourself to the employer in the best possible light.
Your response to this should be well rehearsed, confident and relevant.
Focus on information about yourself that relates to the position.
Be sure to identify your key skills/strengths.
Focus on what you know they are looking for, even if it has only been a small part of what you have done to date.

2. Tell me a time when you had to work under pressure

Your interviewer is encouraging you to talk about a project or piece of work that you found quite stressful. Be clear to show how you dealt with the pressure?
Focus on showing how you found the solution, how you implemented it or took action.
Giving up and walking away are not good responses

The panel wants to learn about your resilience when under stress and how you cope when things go wrong. Emotional intelligence skills come in handy here.

3. Tell me about a time you had to resolve conflict

Again emotional intelligence skills come into play here.
The interviewer wants to know if you can deal with issues within a team.
Describe briefly the structure of the team and your role within it.
If there was conflict, show how you dealt with it and show a positive outcome.

4. Why do you think you are the best candidate for this job?

Explain your motivation for applying for the role, what you know about the company and why you think you are suitable for the position.
Knowing as much as possible about the company will ensure that your explain as best as possible or show how you will add value. Your answer should reinforce why you are a good fit for the job and convey your enthusiasm for the role.
You can mention the good match between your skills, experience and educational qualifications and what the job requires - including what you will bring to the company; your interest in the organisation's area of business/products and the job being an exciting challenge for you.

5. Where do you see yourself in 5 years?

Your interviewer wants to know how the job you are going for fits in with your long-term plans.
You have a clear response of what you hope to have achieved in five years with relates with the job. For example, for an academic position this would include upgrading your qualifications, both academic and professional (including e-learning), contributing to scholarship and engaging in community service.

Tell the interviewer how the job and their organisation fits in with these ideas.

Remember to be precise. Avoid stammering.

6. What is the vision/mission statement of the organisation and how does it link with your skills?

You should demonstrate evidence of having done research by reciting the organization's mission and vision. Furthermore you should be able to identify how you can achieve the mission through your abilities or skills.

7. What are your weaknesses?

Many people are not sure how to answer this question. Remember that all people have weaknesses and that when interviewers ask this question, they are testing self awareness and want to know what your development needs are. For this reason be sure to know yourself.

NB For every weakness you provide, have a strategy to manage it.

It is important to provide a weakness that does not make you appear as not the best candidate for the job. For example- *You may state that your weakness is wanting to be perfect in every task you do, such that you end up completing assignments very close to the deadline.*

Remember to acknowledge that improving on your 'weaknesses' is important to you and, where possible, show how you are working to develop them. For example, you might be someone who is shy, but you purposefully make an effort to talk to people as you recognise this is an issue.

8. If you are successful when do you think you can start

This depends from person to person. Your answer may include specifying how much notice you will need to give your present employer. A lot of organisations are usually flexible unless if the position is an immediate one (If you are flexible to start any time, you have to say).

26.3   Common Mistakes at Interviews

Showing lack of confidence
Being unsure about what the organisation does
Allowing nerves to take over
Failing to answer convincingly

26.4   What to Avoid at Interviews

- Bringing coffee or gum
- Having your phone on
- Interview nerves
- Short sleeved shirts
- Slang and unprofessional language
- Generic answers- give as many examples as possible of different situations.
- Speaking negatively about your previous employer. **NB.**Remember companies are looking for problem solvers.
- Pretending to be someone else

26.5   Final tips

- Take time to prepare well in advance
- Research about the organisation as you will need to use the information to show how it links with your interests and goals and also show the strengths you have to achieve their mission
- Practice makes perfect, the more you practice, the more self assured you will be when you get to the interview
- Remember that this is your only opportunity so nail it.

References

1. Doyle, A. 2018. Learn how to Ace a Job interview https://www.thebalancecareers.com/job-interviews-4161912Accessed 12 April 2019
2. Seager, C. 2016. Four top tips for interview success. https://www.theguardian.com/careers/2016/aug/23/ultimate-top-tips-for-job-interview-success 23 August 2016. Accessed 12 April 2019
3. Succeeding in interviews https://www.cipd.co.uk/new-hr-learning-development/job-guides/succeeding-interviewsAccessed 12 April 2019
4. Von der Heydt 2013. https://www.linkedin.com/pulse/20130912053712-175081329-how-you-succeed-at-every-job-interview/ 12 September 2013.

Chapter 27

Other Important Things to be done

26. Networking

The world we live in requires you to network as much as possible. Whether online or offline, you should build relationships with others based on sharing information and opportunities. Through networking you will find the step to your next destination. Participating in events is important for networking. You should attend workshops, seminars, conferences and meetings on issues related to your field and also outside. Networking will also enable you to see the world differently and to strive to reach your next best level.

27.1 Brand Yourself

It is important to know who you are; your values and mission. You should also understand how other people perceive you. If you have an online presence and have a following, post content that is in line with what you stand for. Upload content regularly and engage your followers on the issues you care about. Always be sincere and kind to your followers. Do not get angry when people post comments on your profile that you did not expect. Instead, do some introspection and respond kindly. As stated in the Chapter on ICT skills, do not post offensive and hateful content. Exhibit positive energy at all times.

27.2 Travelling

Travelling is important for you to get out of your comfort zone. You should challenge yourself to go to places you have never been so that you learn about other people's cultures, acquire opportunities for career development and business opportunities and to broaden your horizon. Get out of the habit of bemoaning about your problems, your background or where you are because you can change your situation for the better if you stand up and go out.

27.3   Learning a new language

Globalisation and technological advancements have brought about multiculturalism as people are migrating from one place to another. Travelling will provide you with the opportunity to meet new people and learn their language. You can also learn new languages online for free and at very minimal costs. Employers are looking for people who demonstrate skills that include taking initiative and learning a new language is a part of it.

27.4   Volunteering

You may never know where and how your next opportunity will come from. Volunteering is important as it will give you a sense of purpose by enabling you to offer your time and effort to help a worthwhile cause without expecting to be paid. You will also get an opportunity to network with others of like-minded interests and sharpen skills such as communication, leadership, teamwork among others.

27.5   Believe in the Higher Power

Whatever you do, do not compromise on your spirituality. If you believe in the Higher Power, be a strong believer, meditate on God's promises and always be thankful. Stay committed.

27.6   Final Words

The journey to success will not be easy. It requires individuals who will not give up. I am still in that journey with more determination. Individuals who take initiative and who will remain calm in the middle of a storm are the ones who will go higher and higher. The skills that have been identified above are important if you are to make a meaningful contribution and be successful in this 21st Century and beyond.

Sipho Dube
10 Paper Road • Milltown• (268) 123-1234 • siphon.dube@email.com

ACCOUNTING MANAGER

Highly organised and diligent professional drawing upon ten years of experience in accounting and finance to contribute to smooth and productive operations.

-Key skills -

- Bookkeeping: AP, AR, Account Reconciliations, Payroll
- Oral and Written Communications
- Federal and State Tax Preparation
- Office Administration
- Positive Teamwork and Collaboration
- QuickBooks and Microsoft Office Suite

PROFESSIONAL EXPERIENCE

Green Professional Accounting Services

Practice Manager (October 2014 – Present)

Handle and optimize all administrative operations for 7-physician medical practice. Scope of responsibilities includes: accounts receivable / payable, accounting, budget review, and preparation of financials for CPA. *Selected Contributions:*

Eliminated backlog in financial reporting responsibilities within **25 days of initial hiring**.

- Successfully project-managed acquisition and installation of state-of-the-art healthcare billing software that reduced errors **by 30%.**

Bluemills Hardware

Accountant (August 2008 – October 2014)

Skillfully performed all office accounting tasks for small hardware store. Gathered and analyzed financial data, and processed accounts payable, accounts receivable, and payroll for workforce of 35 personnel. *Selected Contributions:*

- Created monthly and annual budget and forecast reports that contributed to a **5% decrease in annual expenditures**.
- Migrated accounting system to a new software provider and integrated all accounting, bookkeeping, tax, and payroll functions into the new system.

EDUCATION & CREDENTIALS

Vermont State College, Rutland, VT

Bachelor of Science in Accounting, 2007

Graduated Magna cum Laude

Curriculum Vitae for Sihle Sibanda

Contact information, including home address, cellphone number, email address and Linked In URL

Brief personal statement (2-3 lines)
  Academic qualifications
  Work Experience
  Publications (if any)
  Key skills
  Community Service
  Hobbies
  References

Made in the USA
Monee, IL
01 October 2021

79009157R10109